PHRASEBOOK
FRENCH

PHRASEBOOK AA
FRENCH

English edition prepared by First Edition Translations Ltd,
Great Britain
Designed and produced by AA Publishing
First published in 1995 as Wat & Hoe Frans,
© Kosmos Uitgevers B.V. - Utrecht/Antwerpen

This edition © AA Media Limited 2005
Reprinted January and October 2006, June 2007,
April and September 2008, October 2009, October 2010,
April 2011

Published by AA Publishing (a trading name of AA Media Limited,
whose registered office is Fanum House, Basing View, Basingstoke,
Hampshire RG21 4EA. Registered number 06112600).

Typeset by Information Engineers, Cambridge.
Printed and bound in China by Everbest.

Find out more about AA Publishing by visiting our website at
theAA.com/shop

A04617

Contents

5 On the road 63–81

6 Public transport 82–93

7 Overnight accommodation 94–105

8 Money matters 106–109

9 Post and telephone 110–116

Introduction

● **Welcome to the AA's essential Phrase Books series**, covering
the most popular European languages and containing everything
you'd expect from a comprehensive language series. They're
concise, accessible and easy to understand, and you'll find them
indispensable on your trip abroad.

Each guide is divided into 15 themed sections and starts with a
pronunciation table which gives you the phonetic spelling to all the
words and phrases you'll need to know for your trip, while at the
back of the book is an extensive word list and grammar guide which
will help you construct basic sentences in your chosen language.

Throughout the book you'll come across coloured boxes with a
beside them. These are designed to help you if you can't understand
what your listener is saying to you. Hand the book over to them and
encourage them to point to the appropriate answer to the question
you are asking.

Other coloured boxes in the book – this time without the symbol –
give alphabetical listings of themed words with their English
translations beside them.

For extra clarity, we have put all English words and phrases in black,
foreign language terms in brown and their phonetic pronunciation in
italic.

This phrase book covers all subjects you are likely to come across
during the course of your visit, from reserving a room for the night to
ordering food and drink at a restaurant and what to do if your car
breaks down or you lose your traveller's cheques and money. With
over 2,000 commonly used words and essential phrases at your
fingertips you can rest assured that you will be able to get by in all
situations, so let the essential Phrase Book become your passport to
6 a secure and enjoyable trip!

Pronunciation table

The pronunciation provided should be read as if it were English, bearing in mind the following main points:

Vowels

a, à or â	a in man	ah	table	tahbl
é	like a in make	ay	été	aytay
è, ê, e	like ai in air	eh	rêve	rehv
e	sometimes like u in fluff	uh	le, ne, je, me	luh, nuh, jhuh, muh
i	like ee in seen	ee	si	see
ô	like o in foam	oa	hôtel	oatehl
o	like o in John	o	homme	om
	sometimes like ô	oa	arroser	ahroasay
u	between ee and ew	ew	tu	tew

Combinations of letters which represent vowel sounds:

ez, er	similar to é	ay	louer	looay
ais, ait	the eh sound	eh	fait	feh
au, eau	similar to ô	oa	beau	boa
ail	like i in side	ahy	travail	trahvahy
ei	similar to è	eh	Seine	sehn
eille	eh + y as in yes	ehy	bouteille	bootehy
eu	similar to e above	uh	feu	fuh
iè	ye as in yes	yeh	siècle	syehkl
ié, ier, iez	y + the ay sound	yay	janvier	jhohnvyay
ille	ee + y as in yes	eey	famille	fameey
oi, oy	combines w + a	wah	moi	mwah
ou, oû	oo as in hoot	oo	vous	voo
ui	combines w and ee	wee	cuir	kweer

7

Consonants

ch	like **sh** in **sh**ine	*sh*	**chaud**	*shoa*
ç	like **s** in **s**ome	*s*	**garçon**	*gahrsawn*
g	before **e**, **i** and **y**			
	like **s** in lei**s**ure	*jh*	**nager**	*nahjhay*
	before **a**, **o** and **u**			
	like **g** in **g**ot	*g*	**gâteau**	*gahtoa*
gn	like **ny** in ca**ny**on	*ny*	**agneau**	*ahnyoa*
h	silent			
j	like **s** in lei**s**ure	*jh*	**jour**	*jhoor*
qu	like **k** in **k**ind	*k*	**que**	*kuh*
r	rolled at the back of the throat			
w	like **v** in **v**ine	*v*	**wagonlit**	*vahgawnlee*

Nasal sounds

Nasal sounds are written in French by adding an n to a vowel or a combination of vowels pronounced as the English ng:

an/am, en/em	a little like **song**	*ohn*	**français**, **lentement**	*frohnseh*, *lohntmohn*
in/im, ain, aim, ein	a little like **bang**	*ahn*	**instant**, **faim**	*ahnstohn*, *fahn*
on/om	a nasal form of **awn**	*awn*	**non**	*nawn*
un/um	a little like **rung**	*uhn*	**un**	*uhn*
ien	**y** + the **ahn** sound	*yahn*	**bien**	*byahn*

1 Useful lists

1.1 Today or tomorrow?

What day is it today? __	C'est quel jour aujourd'hui?
	seh kehl jhoor oajhoordwee?
Today's Monday _____	Aujourd'hui c'est lundi
	oajhoordwee seh luhndee
– Tuesday _____	Aujourd'hui c'est mardi
	oajhoordwee seh mahrdee
– Wednesday _____	Aujourd'hui c'est mercredi
	oajhoordwee seh mehrkruhdee
– Thursday_____	Aujourd'hui c'est jeudi
	oajhoordwee seh jhuhdee
– Friday _____	Aujourd'hui c'est vendredi
	oajhoordwee seh vohndruhdee
– Saturday _____	Aujourd'hui c'est samedi
	oajhoordwee seh sahmdee
– Sunday _____	Aujourd'hui c'est dimanche
	oajhoordwee seh deemohnsh
in January _____	en janvier
	ohn jhohnvyay
since February _____	depuis février
	duhpwee fayvryay
in spring_____	au printemps
	oa prahntohn
in summer _____	en été; l'été
	ohn naytay; laytay
in autumn_____	en automne
	ohn noatonn
in winter _____	en hiver; l'hiver
	ohn neevehr; leevehr
1998 _____	mille neuf cent quatre-vingt-dix-huit
	meel nuhf sohn kahtr vahn dee zweet
the twentieth century___	le vingtième siècle
	luh vahntyehm syehkl
What's the date today?_	Quelle est la date aujourd'hui?
	kehl eh lah daht oajhoordwee?

Today's the 24th _____	Aujourd'hui on est le vingt-quatre
	oajhoordwee awn neh luh vahnkahtr
Monday 3 November ___ 1997	lundi, le trois novembre 1997
	luhndee, luh trwah novohnbr meel nuhf sohn kahtr vahn dee seht
in the morning _____	le matin
	luh mahtahn
in the afternoon _____	l'après-midi
	lahpreh meedee
in the evening _____	le soir
	luh swahr
at night _____	la nuit
	lah nwee
this morning _____	ce matin
	suh mahtahn
this afternoon _____	cet après-midi
	seht ahpreh meedee
this evening _____	ce soir
	suh swahr
tonight _____	ce soir
	suh swahr
last night _____	hier soir
	yehr swahr
this week _____	cette semaine
	seht suhmehn
next month _____	le mois prochain
	luh mwah proshahn
last year _____	l'année passée
	lahnay pahsay
next... _____	prochain/prochaine
	proshahn/proshehn
in...days/weeks/ months/years _____	dans...jours/semaines/mois/ans
	dohn...jhoor/suhmehn/mwah/ohn
...weeks ago _____	il y a...semaines
	eel ee ah...suhmehn
day off _____	jour de congé
	jhoor duh kawnjhay

1.2 Bank holidays

● **The most important** Bank holidays in France are the following:

January 1	Le Jour de l'An (New Year's Day)
March/April	Pâques, (Easter)
	le lundi de Pâques (Easter Monday)
May 1	La Fête du Travail (May Day; Labour Day)
May 8	Le Jour de la Libération (Liberation Day)
May/June	L'Ascension; la Pentecôte (Ascension; Whit Sunday)
July 14	La Fête Nationale (Bastille Day)
August 15	L'Assomption (Assumption)
November 1	La Toussaint (All Saints' Day)
November 11	L'Armistice (Armistice Day)
December 25	Noël (Christmas)

Most shops, banks and government institutions are closed on these days. Banks close the afternoon before a Bank holiday and some banks close on Mondays in the provinces. Good Friday and Boxing Day are not Bank Holidays

1.3 What time is it?

What time is it? _____	**Quelle heure est-il?**
	kehl uhr eh teel?
It's nine o'clock _____	**Il est neuf heures**
	eel eh nuh vuhr
– five past ten _____	**Il est dix heures cinq**
	eel eh dee zuhr sahnk
– a quarter past eleven _	**Il est onze heures et quart**
	eel eh tawnz uhr ay kahr
– twenty past twelve ___	**Il est douze heures vingt**
	eel eh dooz uhr vahn
– half past one _____	**Il est une heure et demie**
	eel eh tewn uhr ay duhmee

12

English	French
– twenty–five to three	Il est trois heures moins vingt-cinq
	eel eh trwah zuhr mwahn vahn sahnk
– a quarter to four	Il est quatre heures moins le quart
	eel eh kahtr uhr mwahn luh kahr
– ten to five	Il est cinq heures moins dix
	eel eh sahnk uhr mwahn dees
– twelve noon	Il est midi
	eel eh meedee
– midnight	Il est minuit
	eel eh meenwee
half an hour	une demi-heure
	ewn duhmee uhr
What time?	A quelle heure?
	ah kehl uhr?
What time can I come round?	A quelle heure puis-je venir?
	ah kehl uhr pwee jhuh vuhneer?
At...	A...
	ah...
After...	Après...
	ahpreh...
Before...	Avant...
	ahvohn...
Between...and...	Entre...et...
	ohntr...ay...
From...to...	De...à...
	duh...ah...
In...minutes	Dans...minutes
	dohn...meenewt
– an hour	Dans une heure
	dohn zewn uhr
– ...hours	Dans...heures
	dohn...uhr
– a quarter of an hour	Dans un quart d'heure
	dohn zuhn kahr duhr
– three quarters of an hour	Dans trois quarts d'heure
	dohn trwah kahr duhr

early/late	_____	trop tôt/tard
		troa toa/tahr
on time	_____	à temps
		ah tohn
summertime	_____	l'heure d'été
		luhr daytay
wintertime	_____	l'heure d'hiver
		luhr deevehr

1.4 One, two, three...

0	_____	zéro	_zayroa_
1	_____	un	_uhn_
2	_____	deux	_duh_
3	_____	trois	_trwah_
4	_____	quatre	_kahtr_
5	_____	cinq	_sahnk_
6	_____	six	_sees_
7	_____	sept	_seht_
8	_____	huit	_weet_
9	_____	neuf	_nuhf_
10	_____	dix	_dees_
11	_____	onze	_awnz_
12	_____	douze	_dooz_
13	_____	treize	_trehz_
14	_____	quatorze	_kahtorz_
15	_____	quinze	_kahnz_
16	_____	seize	_sehz_
17	_____	dix-sept	_dee seht_
18	_____	dix-huit	_dee zweet_
19	_____	dix-neuf	_deez nuhf_
20	_____	vingt	_vahn_
21	_____	vingt et un	_vahn tay uhn_
22	_____	vingt-deux	_vahn duh_

30 _____	trente	*trohnt*
31 _____	trente et un	*trohn tay uhn*
32 _____	trente-deux	*trohnt duh*
40 _____	quarante	*kahrohnt*
50 _____	cinquante	*sahnkohnt*
60 _____	soixante	*swahssohnt*
70 _____	soixante-dix	*swahssohnt dees*
80 _____	quatre-vingts	*kahtr vahn*
90 _____	quatre-vingt-dix	*kahtr vahn dees*
100 _____	cent	*sohn*
101 _____	cent un	*sohn uhn*
110 _____	cent dix	*sohn dees*
120 _____	cent vingt	*sohn vahn*
200 _____	deux cents	*duh sohn*
300 _____	trois cents	*trwah sohn*
400 _____	quatre cents	*kahtr sohn*
500 _____	cinq cents	*sahnk sohn*
600 _____	six cents	*see sohn*
700 _____	sept cents	*seht sohn*
800 _____	huit cents	*wee sohn*
900 _____	neuf cents	*nuhf sohn*
1,000 _____	mille	*meel*
1,100 _____	mille cent	*meel sohn*
2,000 _____	deux mille	*duh meel*
10,000 _____	dix mille	*dee meel*
100,000 _____	cent mille	*sohn meel*
1,000,000 _____	un million	*uhn meelyawn*
1st _____	le premier	*luh pruhmyay*
2nd _____	le deuxième	*luh duhzyehm*
3rd _____	le troisième	*luh trwahzyehm*
4th _____	le quatrième	*luh kahtryehm*
5th _____	le cinquième	*luh sahnkyehm*
6th _____	le sixième	*luh seezyehm*
7th _____	le septième	*luh sehtyehm*
8th _____	le huitième	*luh weetyehm*

9th	le neuvième	*luh nuhvyehm*
10th	le dixième	*luh deezyehm*
11th	le onzième	*luh awnzyehm*
12th	le douzième	*luh doozyehm*
13th	le treizième	*luh trehzyehm*
14th	le quatorzième	*luh kahtorzyehm*
15th	le quinzième	*luh kahnzyehm*
16th	le seizième	*luh sehzyehm*
17th	le dix-septième	*luh dee sehtyehm*
18th	le dix-huitième	*luh dee zweetyehm*
19th	le dix-neuvième	*luh deez nuhvyehm*
20th	le vingtième	*luh vahntyehm*
21st	le vingt et unième	*luh vahn tay-ewnyehm*
22nd	le vingt-deuxième	*luh vahn duhzyehm*
30th	le trentième	*luh trohntyehm*
100th	le centième	*luh sohntyehm*
1,000th	le millième	*luh meelyehm*

once	une fois	*ewn fwah*
twice	deux fois	*duh fwah*
double	le double	*luh doobl*
triple	le triple	*luh treepl*
half	la moitié	*lah mwahtyay*
a quarter	un quart	*uhn kahr*
a third	un tiers	*uhn tyehr*

a couple, a few, some __ quelques, un nombre de, quelques
kehlkuh, uhn nawnbr duh, kehlkuh

$2 + 4 = 6$ deux plus quatre égalent six
duh plews kahtr aygahl sees

$4 - 2 = 2$ quatre moins deux égalent deux
kahtr mwahn duh aygahl duh

$2 \times 4 = 8$ deux fois quatre égalent huit
duh fwah kahtr aygahl weet

$4 \div 2 = 2$ quatre divisé par deux égalent deux
kahtr deeveezay pahr duh aygahl duh

odd/even _____	impair/pair
	ahnpehr/pehr
total_____	(au) total
	(oa) totahl
6 x 9 _____	six fois neuf
	see fwah nuhf

1.5 The weather

Is the weather going ___ to be good/bad?	Va-t-il faire beau/mauvais?
	vah teel fehr boa/moaveh?
Is it going to get_____ colder/hotter?	Va-t-il faire plus froid/plus chaud?
	vah teel fehr plew frwah/plew shoa?
What temperature is it__ going to be?	Quelle température va-t-il faire?
	Kehl tohnpayrahtewr vah teel fehr?
Is it going to rain? _____	Va-t-il pleuvoir?
	vah teel pluhvwahr?
Is there going to be a __ storm?	Va-t-il faire de la tempête?
	vah teel fehr duh lah tohnpeht?
Is it going to snow?_____	Va-t-il neiger?
	vah teel nehjhay?
Is it going to freeze? ___	Va-t-il geler?
	vah teel jhuhlay?
Is the thaw setting in?__	Va-t-il dégeler?
	vah teel dayjhuhlay?
Is it going to be foggy?_	Y aura-t-il du brouillard?
	ee oarah teel dew brooy-yahr?
Is there going to be a __ thunderstorm?	Va-t-il faire de l'orage?
	vah teel fehr duh lorahjh?
The weather's _____ changing	Le temps change
	luh tohn shohnjh
It's cooling down _____	Ça se rafraîchit
	sah suh rahfrehshee

What's the weather _____ going to be like today/tomorrow?

Quel temps va-t-il faire aujourd'hui/demain?

kehl tohn vah teel fehr oajhoordwee/duhmahn?

nuageux cloudy	**pluvieux** raining	**les rafales de vent** squalls
beau fine	**la canicule** scorching hot	**l'ouragan (m.)** hurricane
chaud hot	**la grêle** hail	**lourd** muggy
...degrés (au-dessous/au-dessus de zéro) ...degrees (below/above zero)	**la neige** snow	**l'orage (m.)** thunderstorm
	la pluie rain	**orageux** stormy
couvert overcast	**la vague de chaleur** heatwave	**pénétrant** bleak
le crachin drizzle	**l'averse (f.)** shower	**ciel dégagé** clear
doux mild	**le brouillard** fog	**brumeux** misty
ensoleillé sunny	**le gel** ice	**vent faible/modéré/fort** light/moderate/strong wind
frais chilly	**le vent** wind	
froid cold	**le verglas** black ice	**venteux** windy
humide damp	**les nuages** clouds	

1.6 Here, there...

See also 5.1 Asking for directions

here/there _____ **ici/là**
eesee/lah

somewhere/nowhere ___ **quelque part/nulle part**
kehlkuh pahr/newl pahr

everywhere _____ **partout**
pahrtoo

far away/nearby _____ **loin/à côté**
lwahn/ah koatay

right/left _____ **la droite/la gauche**
lah drwaht/lah goash

to the right/left of _____ **à droite de/à gauche de**
ah drwaht duh/ah goash duh

straight ahead_____ **tout droit**
too drwah

via _____ **par**
pahr

in _____ **dans**
dohn

on _____ **sur**
sewr

under _____ **sous**
soo

against _____ **contre**
kawntr

opposite_____ **en face de**
ohn fahs duh

next to _____ **à côté de**
ah koatay duh

near_____ **près de**
preh duh

in front of_____ **devant**
devohn

in the centre _____ au milieu de
oa meelyuh duh

forward_____ en avant
ohn nahvohn

down_____ en bas
ohn bah

up _____ en haut
ohn oa

inside _____ à l'intérieur
ah lahntayryuhr

outside _____ à l'extérieur
ah lehxtayryuhr

behind _____ derrière
dehryehr

at the front_____ à l'avant
ah lahvohn

at the back _____ à l'arrière
ah lahryehr

in the north _____ au nord
oa nor

to the south_____ vers le sud
vehr luh sewd

from the west _____ venant de l'ouest
vuhnohn duh lwehst

from the east_____ venant de l'est
vuhnohn duh lehst

1.7 What does that sign say?

See also 5.4 Traffic signs

à louer
for hire

à vendre
for sale

accueil
reception

animaux interdits
no pets allowed

ascenseur
lift

attention à la
  marche
mind the step

attention chien
  méchant
beware of the dog

caisse
pay here

complet
full

dames
ladies

danger
danger

défense de toucher
please do not touch

eau non potable
no drinking water

en panne
out of order

entrée
entrance

entrée gratuite
admission free

entrée interdite
no entry

escalier roulant
escalator

escalier
stairs

escalier de secours
fire escape

...étage
...floor

frein de secours
emergency brake

haute tension
high voltage

heures d'ouverture
opening hours

interdit d'allumer un
  feu
no open fires

interdit de fumer
no smoking

interdit de
  photographier
no photographs

liquidation de stock
closing-down sale

messieurs
gents/gentlemen

ne pas déranger s'il
  vous plaît
do not disturb please

ouvert/fermé
open/closed

peinture fraîche
wet paint

pelouse interdite
keep off the grass

premiers soins
first aid

propriété privée
private (property)

renseignements
information

réservé
reserved

risque d'incendie
fire hazard

soldes
sale

sortie
exit

sortie de secours
emergency exit

pousser/tirer
push/pull

toilettes, wc
toilets

21

1.8 Telephone alphabet

a	*ah*	comme Anatole	*kom ahnnahtol*
b	*bay*	comme Berthe	*kom behrt*
c	*say*	comme Célestin	*kom saylehstahn*
d	*day*	comme Désiré	*kom dayzeeray*
e	*uh*	comme Eugène	*kom uhjhehn*
f	*ehf*	comme François	*kom frohnswah*
g	*jhay*	comme Gaston	*kom gahstawn*
h	*ash*	comme Henri	*kom ohnree*
i	*ee*	comme Irma	*kom eermah*
j	*jhee*	comme Joseph	*kom jhosehf*
k	*kah*	comme Kléber	*kom klaybehr*
l	*ehl*	comme Louis	*kom looee*
m	*ehm*	comme Marcel	*kom mahrsehl*
n	*ehn*	comme Nicolas	*kom neekolah*
o	*oh*	comme Oscar	*kom oskahr*
p	*pay*	comme Pierre	*kom pyehr*
q	*kew*	comme Quintal	*kom kahntahl*
r	*ehr*	comme Raoul	*kom rahool*
s	*ehs*	comme Suzanne	*kom sewzahnn*
t	*tay*	comme Thérèse	*kom tayrehz*
u	*ew*	comme Ursule	*kom ewrsewl*
v	*vee*	comme Victor	*kom veektor*
w	*doobluhvay*	comme William	*kom weelyahm*
x	*eex*	comme Xavier	*kom gsahvyay*
y	*eegrehk*	comme Yvonne	*kom eevon*
z	*zehd*	comme Zoé	*kom zoa-ay*

1.9 Personal details

surname _____	**nom** *nawn*
christian name(s) _____	**prénom(s)** *praynawn*
initials _____	**initiales** *eeneesyahl*
address _____ (street/number)	**adresse (rue/numéro)** *ahdrehs (rew/newmayroa)*
post code/town _____	**code postal/ville** *kod postahl/veel*
sex (male/female) _____	**sexe (m/f)** *sehx (ehm/ehf)*
nationality _____	**nationalité** *nahsyonahleetay*
date of birth_____	**date de naissance** *daht duh nehsohns*
place of birth_____	**lieu de naissance** *lyuh duh nehsohns*
occupation _____	**profession** *profehsyawn*
married/single/ _____ divorced	**marié(e) /célibataire/divorcé(e)** *mahreeay/sayleebahtehr/deevorsay*
widowed _____	**veuf/veuve** *vuhf/vuhv*
(number of) children____	**(nombre d')enfants** *(nawnbr d)ohnfohn*

identity card/passport/ _
  driving licence number
	numéro de carte d'identité/
	  passeport/permis de conduire
	newmayroa duh kahrt deedohnteetay/
	  pahspor/pehrmee duh kawndweer

place and date of_____ issue	**lieu et date de délivrance** *lyuh ay daht duh dayleevrohns*

2 Courtesies

● **It is usual in France** to shake hands on meeting and parting company. Female friends and relatives may kiss each other on both cheeks when meeting and parting company. With men this varies according to the region. It is also polite to say monsieur and madame quite systematically as part of a greeting, i.e. Bonjour, monsieur; au revoir, madame.

● **The English** 'you' is expressed in French by either 'tu' or 'vous'. 'Tu' is the more familiar form of address, used to talk to someone close or used between young people or when adults are talking to young children. 'Vous' is the more formal and polite form of address. 'On' is the generalised form of 'nous' meaning people in general ('one' and 'we' in English).

2.1 Greetings

Hello, Mr Smith _____	**Bonjour monsieur Smith**
	bawnjhoor muhsyuh dewpawn
Hello, Mrs Jones _____	**Bonjour madame Jones**
	bawnjhoor mahdahm dewrohn
Hello, Peter _____	**Salut, Pierre**
	sahlew, pyehr
Hi, Helen _____	**Ça va, Hélène?**
	sah vah, aylehn?
Good morning, madam_	**Bonjour madame**
	bawnjhoor mahdahm
Good afternoon, sir ____	**Bonjour monsieur**
	bawnjhoor muhsyuh
Good evening _____	**Bonsoir**
	bawhnswahr
How are you? _____	**Comment allez-vous?**
	komohn tahlay voo?
Fine, thank you, _____ and you?	**Très bien et vous?**
	treh byahn ay voo?
Very well_____	**Très bien**
	treh byahn

Not very well	**Pas très bien**
	pah treh byahn
Not too bad	**Ça va**
	sah vah
I'd better be going	**Je m'en vais**
	jhuh mohn veh
I have to be going	**Je dois partir**
	jhuh dwah pahrteer
Someone's waiting for me	**On m'attend**
	awn mahtohn
Bye!	**Salut!**
	sahlew!
Goodbye	**Au revoir**
	oa ruhvwahr
See you soon	**A bientôt**
	ah byahntoa
See you later	**A tout à l'heure**
	ah too tah luhr
See you in a little while	**A tout de suite**
	ah toot sweet
Sleep well	**Dormez bien/dors bien**
	dormay byahn, dor byahn
Good night	**Bonne nuit**
	bon nwee
Have fun	**Amuse-toi bien**
	ahmewz twah byahn
Good luck	**Bonne chance**
	bon shahns
Have a nice holiday	**Bonnes vacances**
	bon vahkohns
Have a good trip	**Bon voyage**
	bawn vwahyahjh
Thank you, you too	**Merci, de même**
	mehrsee, duh mehm
Say hello to...for me	**Mes amitiés à...**
	may zahmeetyay ah...

2.2 How to ask a question

Who? _____	**Qui?**
	kee?
Who's that? _____	**Qui est-ce?**
	kee ehs?
What? _____	**Quoi?**
	kwah?
What's there to _____ see here?	**Qu'est-ce qu'on peut voir ici?**
	kehsk awn puh vwahr eesee?
What kind of hotel _____ is that?	**C'est quelle sorte d'hôtel?**
	seh kehl sort doatehl?
Where? _____	**Où?**
	oo?
Where's the toilet? _____	**Où sont les toilettes?**
	oo sawn lay twahleht?
Where are you going? __	**Où allez-vous?**
	oo ahlay voo?
Where are you from? ___	**D'où venez-vous?**
	doo vuhnay voo?
How? _____	**Comment?**
	komohn?
How far is that? _____	**C'est loin?**
	seh lwahn?
How long does that ____ take?	**Combien de temps faut-il?**
	kawnbyahn duh tohn foa teel?
How long is the trip? ___	**Combien de temps dure le voyage?**
	kawnbyahn duh tohn dewr luh vwahyahjh?
How much? _____	**Combien?**
	kawnbyahn?
How much is this? _____	**C'est combien?**
	seh kawnbyahn?
What time is it? _____	**Quelle heure est-il?**
	kehl uhr eh teel?
Which? _____	**Quel? Quels?/Quelle? Quelles?**
	kehl?

Which glass is mine? ___	**Quel est mon verre?** *kehl eh mawn vehr?*
When? ___	**Quand?** *kohn?*
When are you leaving? _	**Quand partez-vous?** *kohn pahrtay voo?*
Why? ___	**Pourquoi?** *poorkwah?*
Could you...me? ___	**Pouvez-vous me...?** *poovay voo muh...?*
Could you help me, ___ please?	**Pouvez-vous m'aider s'il vous plaît?** *poovay voo mayday seel voo pleh?*
Could you point that ___ out to me?	**Pouvez-vous me l'indiquer?** *poovay voo muh lahndeekay?*
Could you come___ with me, please?	**Pouvez-vous m'accompagner s'il vous plaît?** *poovay voo mahkawnpahnnyay seel voo pleh?*
Could you...___	**Voulez-vous...?** *voolay voo...?*
Could you reserve ___ some tickets for me, please?	**Voulez-vous me réserver des places s'il vous plaît?** *voolay voo muh rayzehrvay day plahs seel voo pleh?*
Do you know...? ___	**Connaissez-vous...?** *konehssay voo...?*
Do you know another _ hotel, please?	**Vous connaissez peut-être un autre hôtel?** *voo konehssay puh tehtr uhn noatr oatehl?*
Do you know whether...?___	**Savez-vous si...?** *sahvay voo see...?*
Do you have a...?___	**Avez-vous un...?** *ahvay voo zuhn...?*
Do you have a ___ vegetarian dish, please?	**Vous avez peut-être un plat sans viande?** *voo zahvay puh tehtr uhn plah sohn vyohnd?*

I'd like... _____	**Je voudrais...**
	jhuh voodreh...
I'd like a kilo of apples, _ please	**Je voudrais un kilo de pommes**
	jhuh voodreh zuhn keeloa duh pom
Can I...? _____	**Puis-je...?**
	pwee jhuh...?
Can I take this? _____	**Puis-je prendre ceci?**
	pwee jhuh prohndr suhsee?
Can I smoke here?_____	**Puis-je fumer ici?**
	pwee jhuh fewmay eesee?
Could I ask you _____ something?	**Puis-je vous demander quelque chose?**
	pwee jhuh voo duhmohnday kehlkuh shoaz?

2.3 How to reply

Yes, of course_____	**Oui, bien sûr**
	wee, byahn sewr
No, I'm sorry _____	**Non, je suis désolé**
	nawn, jhuh swee dayzolay
Yes, what can I do _____ for you?	**Oui, que puis-je faire pour vous?**
	wee, kuh pwee jhuh fehr poor voo?
Just a moment, please _	**Un moment s'il vous plaît**
	uhn momohn seel voo pleh
No, I don't have _____ time now	**Non, je n'ai pas le temps en ce moment**
	nawn, jhuh nay pah luh tohn ohn suh momohn
No, that's impossible___	**Non, c'est impossible**
	nawn, seh tahnposseebl
I think so _____	**Je le crois bien**
	jhuh luh krwah byahn
I agree _____	**Je le pense aussi**
	jhuh luh pohns oasee
I hope so too_____	**Je l'espère aussi**
	jhuh lehspehr oasee

No, not at all _____	**Non, absolument pas**
	nawn, ahbsolewmohn pah
No, no-one _____	**Non, personne**
	nawn, pehrson
No, nothing _____	**Non, rien**
	nawn, ryahn
That's (not) right _____	**C'est (ce n'est pas) exact**
	seht (suh neh pahz) ehgzah
I (don't) agree _____	**Je suis (je ne suis pas) d'accord avec**
	vous
	jhuh swee (jhuh nuh swee pah) dahkor
	ahvehk voo
All right_____	**C'est bien** *seh byahn*
Okay _____	**D'accord** *dahkor*
Perhaps _____	**Peut-être** *puh tehtr*
I don't know _____	**Je ne sais pas** *jhuh nuh seh pah*

2.4 Thank you

Thank you _____	**Merci/merci bien**
	mehrsee/mehrsee byahn
You're welcome _____	**De rien/avec plaisir**
	duh ryahn/ahvehk playzeer
Thank you very much __	**Merci beaucoup**
	mehrsee boakoo
Very kind of you _____	**C'est aimable de votre part**
	seh taymahbl duh votr pahr
I enjoyed it very much__	**C'était un réel plaisir**
	sayteh tuhn rayehl playzeer
Thank you for your_____	**Je vous remercie pour la peine**
trouble	*jhuh voo ruhmehrsee poor lah pehn*
You shouldn't have ____	**Vous n'auriez pas dû**
	voo noaryay pah dew
That's all right _____	**Pas de problème**
	pah duh problehm

2.5 Sorry

|---|---|
Excuse me	**Excusez-moi** *ehxkewzay mwah*
Sorry!	**Pardon!** *pahrdawn!*
I'm sorry, I didn't know...	**Pardon, je ne savais pas que...** *pahrdawn jhuh nuh sahveh pah kuh...*
I do apologise	**Excusez-moi** *ehxkewzay mwah*
I'm sorry	**Je suis désolé** *jhuh swee dayzolay*
I didn't do it on purpose, it was an accident	**Je ne l'ai pas fait exprès, c'était un accident** *jhuh ne lay pah feh ehxpreh, sayteh tuhn nahxeedohn*
That's all right	**Ce n'est pas grave** *suh neh pah grahv*
Never mind	**Ça ne fait rien** *sah nuh feh ryahn*
It could've happened to anyone	**Ça peut arriver à tout le monde** *sah puh ahreevay ah too luh mawnd*

2.6 What do you think?

Which do you prefer?	**Qu'est-ce que vous préférez?** *kehs kuh voo prayfayray?*
What do you think?	**Qu'en penses-tu?** *kohn pohns tew?*
Don't you like dancing?	**Tu n'aimes pas danser?** *tew nehm pah dohnsay?*
I don't mind	**Ça m'est égal** *sah meh taygahl*
Well done!	**Très bien!** *treh byahn!*
Not bad!	**Pas mal!** *pah mahl!*
Great!	**Génial!** *jhaynyahl!*
Wonderful!	**Super!** *sewpehr!*

It's really nice here! ____	**C'est drôlement agréable ici!**
	seh droalmohn ahgrayahbl eesee!
How nice!_____	**Pas mal, chouette!**
	pah mahl, shweht!
How nice for you!_____	**C'est formidable!**
	seh formeedahbl!
I'm (not) very happy____	**Je suis (ne suis pas) très satisfait(e) de...**
with...	*jhuh swee (nuh swee pah) treh*
	sahteesfeh(t) duh...
I'm glad..._____	**Je suis content(e) que...**
	jhuh swee kawntohn(t) kuh...
I'm having a great time _	**Je m'amuse beaucoup**
	jhuh mahmewz boakoo
I'm looking forward ____	**Je m'en réjouis**
to it	*jhuh mohn rayjhwee*
I hope it'll work out ____	**J'espère que cela réussira**
	jhehspehr kuh suhlah rayewseerah
That's ridiculous! _____	**C'est nul!** *seh newl!*
That's terrible!_____	**Quelle horreur!** *kehl oruhr!*
What a pity!_____	**C'est dommage!** *seh domahjh!*
That's filthy!_____	**C'est dégoûtant!**
	seh daygootohn!
What a load of _____	**C'est ridicule/C'est absurde!**
rubbish!	*seh reedeekewl/seh tahbsewrd!*
I don't like... _____	**Je n'aime pas...**
	jhuh nehm pah...
I'm bored to death _____	**Je m'ennuie à mourir**
	jhuh mohnnwee ah mooreer
I've had enough _____	**J'en ai assez/ras le bol**
	jhohn nay ahsay/rahl bol
This is no good_____	**Ce n'est pas possible**
	suh neh pah posseebl
I was expecting _____	**Je m'attendais à quelque chose de très**
something completely	**différent**
different	*jhuh mahtohndeh ah kehlkuh shoaz duh*
	treh deefayrohn

3 Conversation

3.1 I beg your pardon?

I don't speak any/ _____ I speak a little...	**Je ne parle pas/je parle un peu...** *jhuh nuh pahrl pah/jhuh pahrl uhn puh..*
I'm English_____	**Je suis anglais/anglaise** *jhuh swee zohngleh/zohnglehz*
I'm Scottish_____	**Je suis écossais/écossaise** *jhuh swee zaykosseh/zaykossehz*
I'm Irish _____	**Je suis irlandais/irlandaise** *jhuh swee zeerlohndeh/zeerlohndehz*
I'm Welsh_____	**Je suis gallois/galloise** *jhuh swee gahlwah/gahlwahz*
Do you speak _____ English/French/ German?	**Parlez-vous anglais/français/allemand?** *pahrlay voo ohngleh/ frohnseh/ahlmohn?*
Is there anyone who ___ speaks...?	**Y a-t-il quelqu'un qui parle...?** *ee yah teel kehlkuhn kee pahrl...?*
I beg your pardon? ____	**Que dites-vous?** *kuh deet voo?*
I (don't) understand ____	**Je (ne) comprends (pas)** *jhuh (nuh) kawnprohn (pah)*
Do you understand me?	**Me comprenez-vous?** *me kawnpruhnay voo?*
Could you repeat that, _ please?	**Voulez-vous répéter s'il vous plaît?** *voolay voo raypaytay seel voo pleh?*
Could you speak more _ slowly, please?	**Pouvez-vous parler plus lentement?** *poovay voo pahrlay plew lohntmohn?*
What does that word___ mean?	**Qu'est-ce que ce mot veut dire?** *kehs kuh suh moa vuh deer?*
Is that similar to/the____ same as...?	**Est-ce (environ) la même chose que...?** *ehs (ohnveerawn) lah mehm shoaz kuh...?*
Could you write that ___ down for me, please?	**Pouvez-vous me l'écrire?** *poovay voo muh laykreer?*
Could you spell that ___ for me, please?	**Pouvez-vous me l'épeler?** *poovay voo muh laypuhlay?*

(See 1.8 Telephone alphabet)

Could you point that ___ out in this phrase book, please?	Pouvez-vous me le montrer dans ce guide de conversation? *poovay voo muh luh mawntray dohn suh gueed duh kawnvehrsahsyawn?*
One moment, please, ___ I have to look it up	Un moment, je dois le chercher *uhn momohn, jhuh dwah luh shehrshay*
I can't find the word/the sentence	Je ne trouve pas le mot/la phrase *jhuh nuh troov pah luh moa/lah frahz*
How do you say _____ that in...?	Comment dites-vous cela en...? *komohn deet voo suhlah ohn...?*
How do you _____ pronounce that?	Comment prononcez-vous cela? *komohn pronawnsay voo suhlah?*

3.2 Introductions

May I introduce myself?	Puis-je me présenter? *pwee jhuh muh prayzohntay?*
My name's... _____	Je m'appelle... *jhuh mahpehl...*
I'm... _____	Je suis... *jhuh swee...*
What's your name? ____	Comment vous appelez-vous? *komohn voo zahpuhlay voo?*
May I introduce...? _____	Puis-je vous présenter? *pwee jhuh voo prayzohntay?*
This is my wife/ _____ daughter/mother/ girlfriend	Voici ma femme/fille/mère/mon amie *vwahsee mah fahm/feey/mehr/mawn nahmee*
– my husband/son/ ____ father/boyfriend	Voici mon mari/fils/père/ami *vwahsee mawn mahree/fees/pehr/ahmee*
How do you do_____	Enchanté(e). *ohnshohntay*

Pleased to meet you ___	**Je suis heureux(se) de faire votre connaissance**
	jhuh swee zuhruh(z) duh fehr votr kohnehssohns
Where are you from? ___	**D'où venez-vous?**
	doo vuhnay voo?
I'm from _____ England/Scotland/ Ireland/Wales	**Je viens d'Angleterre/d'Ecosse/d'Irlande/du pays de Galles**
	jhuh vyahn dohngluhtehr/daykos/deerlohnd dew payee duh gahl
What city do you live in? ___	**Vous habitez dans quelle ville?**
	voo zahbeetay dohn kehl veel?
In..., It's near... _____	**A...C'est à côté de...**
	ah...seh tah koatay duh...
Have you been here long? ___	**Etes-vous ici depuis longtemps?**
	eht voo zeesee duhpwee lawntohn?
A few days_____	**Depuis quelques jours**
	depwee kehlkuh jhoor
How long are you staying here?_____	**Combien de temps restez-vous ici?**
	kawnbyahn duh tohn rehstay voo zeesee?
We're (probably) leaving tomorrow/in two weeks	**Nous partirons (probablement) demain/dans quinze jours**
	noo pahrteerawn (probahbluhmohn) duhmahn/dohn kahnz jhoor
Where are you staying?	**Où logez-vous?**
	oo lojhay voo?
In a hotel/an apartment_	**Dans un hôtel/appartement**
	dohn zuhn noatehl/ahpahrtuhmohn
On a camp site_____	**Dans un camping**
	dohn zuhn kohnpeeng
With friends/relatives ___	**Chez des amis/chez de la famille**
	shay day zahmee/shay duh lah fahmeey
Are you here on your own/with your family? ___	**Etes-vous ici seul/avec votre famille?**
	eht voo zeesee suhl/ahvehk votr fahmeey?
I'm on my own _____	**Je suis seul(e)**
	jhuh swee suhl

I'm with my _____ partner/wife/husband	**Je suis avec mon ami(e)/ma femme/mon mari** *jhuh swee zahvehk mawn nahmee/mah fahm/mawn mahree*
– with my family _____	**Je suis avec ma famille** *jhuh swee zahvehk mah fahmeey*
– with relatives _____	**Je suis avec de la famille** *jhuh swee zahvehk duh lah fahmeey*
– with a friend/friends __	**Je suis avec un ami/une amie /des amis** *jhuh swee zahvehk uhn nahmee/ewn ahmee/day zahmee*
Are you married? _____	**Etes-vous marié(e)?** *eht voo mahreeay?*
Do you have a steady __ boyfriend/girlfriend?	**As-tu un petit ami (une petite amie)?** *ah tew uhn puhtee tahmee (ewn puhteet ahmee)?*
That's none of your ____ business	**Cela ne vous regarde pas** *suhlah nuh voo ruhgahrd pah*
I'm married _____	**Je suis marié(e)** *jhuh swee mahreeay*
– single_____	**Je suis célibataire** *jhuh swee sayleebahtehr*
– separated _____	**Je suis séparé(e)** *jhuh swee saypahray*
– divorced _____	**Je suis divorcé(e)** *jhuh swee deevorsay*
– a widow/widower ____	**Je suis veuf/veuve** *jhuh swee vuhf/vuhv*
I live alone/with_____ someone	**J'habite tout(e) seul(e)/avec quelqu'un** *jhahbeet too suhl(toot suhl)/ahvehk kehlkuhn*
Do you have any _____ children/ grandchildren?	**Avez-vous des enfants/petits-enfants?** *ahvay voo day zohnfohn/puhtee zohnfohn?*
How old are you?_____	**Quel âge avez-vous?** *kehl ahjh ahvay voo?*

How old is he/she? ____	**Quel âge a-t-il/a-t-elle?**
	kehl ahjh ah teel/ah tehl?
I'm...years old _____	**J'ai...ans**
	jhay...ohn
He's/she's...years old __	**Il/elle a...ans**
	eel/ehl ah...ohn
What do you do for a __ living?	**Quel est votre métier?**
	kehl eh votr maytyay?
I work in an office_____	**Je travaille dans un bureau**
	jhuh trahvahy dohn zuhn bewroa
I'm a student/ _____ I'm at school	**Je fais des études/je vais à l'école**
	jhuh feh day zaytewd/jhuh veh zah laykol
I'm unemployed _____	**Je suis au chômage**
	jhuh swee zoa shoamajh
I'm retired _____	**Je suis retraité(e)**
	jhuh swee ruhtrehtay
I'm on a disability_____ pension	**Je suis en invalidité**
	jhuh swee zohn nahnvahleedeetay
I'm a housewife _____	**Je suis femme au foyer**
	jhuh swee fahm oa fwahyay
Do you like your job? __	**Votre travail vous plaît?**
	votr trahvahy voo pleh?
Most of the time_____	**Ça dépend**
	sah daypohn
I prefer holidays _____	**J'aime mieux les vacances**
	Jhehm myuh lay vahkohns

3.3 Starting/ending a conversation

Could I ask you _____ something?	**Puis-je vous poser une question?**
	pwee jhuh voo poazay ewn kehstyawn?
Excuse me_____	**Excusez-moi**
	ehxkewsay mwah
Excuse me, could you__ help me?	**Pardon, pouvez-vous m'aider?**
	pahrdawn, poovay voo mayday?

Yes, what's the _____ problem?	Oui, qu'est-ce qui se passe?
	wee, kehs kee suh pahss?
What can I do for you? _	Que puis-je faire pour vous?
	kuh pwee jhuh fehr poor voo?
Sorry, I don't have time_ now	Excusez-moi, je n'ai pas le temps maintenant
	ehxkewzay mwah, jhuh nay pah luh tohn mahntuhnohn
Do you have a light? ___	Vous avez du feu?
	voo zahvay dew fuh?
May I join you? _____	Puis-je m'asseoir à côté de vous?
	pwee jhuh mahsswahr ah koatay duh voo?
Could you take a _____ picture of me/us?	Voulez-vous me/nous prendre en photo?
Press this button.	Appuyez sur ce bouton.
	voolay voo muh/noo prohndr ohn foatoa? ahpweeyay sewr suh bootawn
Leave me alone _____	Laissez-moi tranquille
	laysay mwah trohnkeey
Get lost _____	Fichez le camp
	feeshay luh kohn
Go away or I'll scream _	Si vous ne partez pas, je crie
	see voo nuh pahrtay pah, jhuh kree

3.4 Congratulations and condolences

Happy birthday/many _ happy returns	Bon anniversaire/bonne fête
	bohn nahnneevehrsehr/bon feht
Please accept my _____ condolences	Mes condoléances
	may kawndolayohns
I'm very sorry for you _	Cela me peine beaucoup pour vous
	suhlah muh pehn boakoo poor voo

3.5 A chat about the weather

See also 1.5 The weather

It's so hot/cold today!	Qu'est-ce qu'il fait chaud/froid aujourd'hui!
	kehs keel feh shoa/frwah oajhoordwee!
Nice weather, isn't it?	Il fait beau, n'est-ce pas?
	eel feh boa, nehs pah?
What a wind/storm!	Quel vent/orage!
	kehl vohn/orahjh!
All that rain/snow!	Quelle pluie/neige!
	kehl plwee/nehjh!
All that fog!	Quel brouillard!
	kehl brooy-yahr!
Has the weather been like this for long here?	Fait-il ce temps-là depuis longtemps?
	feh teel suh tohn lah duhpwee lawntohn?
Is it always this hot/cold here?	Fait-il toujours aussi chaud/froid ici?
	feh teel toojhoor oasee shoa/frwah eesee?
Is it always this dry/wet here?	Fait-il toujours aussi sec/humide ici?
	feh teel toojhoor oasee sehk/ewmeed eesee?

3.6 Hobbies

Do you have any hobbies?	Avez-vous des passe-temps?
	ahvay voo day pahs tohn?
I like painting/reading/photography/DIY	J'aime peindre/lire/la photo/le bricolage
	jhehm pahndr/leer/lah foatoa/luh breekolahjh
I like music	J'aime la musique
	jhehm lah mewzeek
I like playing the guitar/piano	J'aime jouer de la guitare/du piano
	jhehm jhooay duh lah gueetahr/dew pyahnoa

I like going to the _____ movies	J'aime aller au cinéma *jhehm ahlay oa seenaymah*
I like travelling/ _____ sport/fishing/walking	J'aime voyager/faire du sport/la pêche/me promener *jhehm vwahyahjhay/fehr dew spor/lah pehsh/ muh promuhnay*

3.7 Being the host(ess)

See also 4 Eating out

Can I offer you a _____ drink?	Puis-je vous offrir quelque chose à boire? *pwee jhuh voo zofreer kehlkuh shoaz ah bwahr?*
What would you like ___ to drink?	Que désires-tu boire? *kuh dayzeer tew bwahr?*
Something non- _____ alcoholic, please.	De préférence quelque chose sans alcool *duh prayfayrohns kehlkuh shoaz sohn zahlkol*
Would you like a_____ cigarette/cigar/to roll your own?	Voulez-vous une cigarette/un cigare/rouler une cigarette? *voolay voo zewn seegahreht/uhn seegahr/roolay ewn seegahreht?*
I don't smoke _____	Je ne fume pas *jhuh nuh fewm pah*

3.8 Invitations

Are you doing anything_ tonight?	Faites-vous quelque chose ce soir? *feht voo kehlkuh shoaz suh swahr?*
Do you have any plans _ for today/this afternoon/tonight?	Avez-vous déjà fait des projets pour aujourd'hui/cet après-midi/ce soir? *ahvay voo dayjhah feh day projheh poor oa-jhoordwee/seht ahpreh meedee/suh swahr?*

Would you like to go ___ out with me?	**Aimeriez-vous sortir avec moi?** *aymuhryay voo sorteer ahvehk mwah?*
Would you like to go ___ dancing with me?	**Aimeriez-vous aller danser avec moi?** *aymuhryay voo zahlay dohnsay ahvehk mwah?*
Would you like to have _ lunch/dinner with me?	**Aimeriez-vous déjeuner/dîner avec moi?** *aymuhryay voo dayjhuhnay/deenay ahvehk mwah?*
Would you like to _____ come to the beach with me?	**Aimeriez-vous aller à la plage avec moi?** *aymuhryay voo zahlay ah lah plahjh ahvehk mwah?*
Would you like to _____ come into town with us?	**Aimeriez-vous aller en ville avec nous?** *aymuhryay voo zahlay ohn veel ahvehk noo?*
Would you like to _____ come and see some friends with us?	**Aimeriez-vous aller chez des amis avec nous?** *aymuhryay voo zahlay shay day zahmee ahvehk noo?*
Shall we dance?_____	**On danse?** *awn dohns?*
– sit at the bar? _____	**On va s'asseoir au bar?** *awn vah saswahr oa bahr?*
– get something to ___ drink?	**On va boire quelque chose?** *awn vah bwahr kehlkuh shoaz?*
– go for a walk/drive? _	**On va marcher un peu/on va faire un tour en voiture?** *awn vah mahrshay uhn puh/awn vah fehr uhn toor ohn vwahtewr?*
Yes, all right_____	**Oui, d'accord** *wee, dahkor*
Good idea _____	**Bonne idée** *bon eeday*
No (thank you) _____	**Non (merci)** *nawn (mehrsee)*
Maybe later _____	**Peut-être tout à l'heure** *puh tehtr too tah luhr*

I don't feel like it	Je n'en ai pas envie
	jhuh nohn nay pah zohnvee
I don't have time	Je n'ai pas le temps
	jhuh nay pah luh tohn
I already have a date	J'ai déjà un autre rendez-vous
	jhay dayjhah uhn noatr rohnday voo
I'm not very good at dancing/volleyball/ swimming	Je ne sais pas danser/jouer au volley/nager
	jhuh nuh seh pah dohnsay/jhooay oa volay/nahjhay

3.9 Paying a compliment

You look wonderful!	Vous avez l'air en pleine forme!
	voo zahvay lehr ohn plehn form!
I like your car!	Quelle belle voiture!
	kehl behl vwahtewr!
I like your ski outfit!	Quelle belle combinaison de ski!
	kehl behl kawnbeenehzawn duh skee!
You're a nice boy/girl	Tu es un garçon/une fille sympathique
	tew eh zuhn gahrsohn/ewn feey sahnpahteek
What a sweet child!	Quel adorable enfant!
	kehl ahdorahbl ohnfohn!
You're a wonderful dancer!	Vous dansez très bien!
	voo dohnsay treh byahn!
You're a wonderful cook!	Vous faites très bien la cuisine!
	voo feht treh byahn lah kweezeen!
You're a terrific soccer player!	Vous jouez très bien au football!
	voo jhooay treh byahn oa footbol!

3.10 Chatting someone up

I like being with you	**J'aime bien être près de toi** *jhehm byahn ehtr preh duh twah*
I've missed you so much	**Tu m'as beaucoup manqué** *tew mah boakoo mohnkay*
I dreamt about you	**J'ai rêvé de toi** *jhay rehvay duh twah*
I think about you all day	**Je pense à toi toute la journée** *jhuh pohns ah twah toot lah jhoornay*
You have such a sweet smile	**Tu souris si gentiment** *tew sooree see jhohnteemohn*
You have such beautiful eyes	**Tu as de si jolis yeux** *tew ah duh see jhoalee zyuh*
I'm in love with you	**Je suis amoureux/se de toi** *jhuh swee zahmooruh(z) duh twah*
I'm in love with you too	**Moi aussi de toi** *mwah oasee duh twah*
I love you	**Je t'aime** *jhuh tehm*
I love you too	**Je t'aime aussi** *jhuh tehm oasee*
I don't feel as strongly about you	**Je n'ai pas d'aussi forts sentiments pour toi** *jhuh nay pah doasee for sohnteemohn poor twah*
I already have a boyfriend/girlfriend	**J'ai déjà un ami/une amie** *jhay dayjhah uhn nahmee/ewn ahmee*
I'm not ready for that	**Je n'en suis pas encore là** *jhuh nohn swee pah zohnkor lah*
This is going too fast for me.	**Ça va un peu trop vite** *sah vah uhn puh troa veet*
Take your hands off me	**Ne me touche pas** *nuh muh toosh pah*

Okay, no problem	**D'accord, pas de problème**
	dahkor, pah duh problehm
Will you stay with me tonight?	**Tu restes avec moi cette nuit?**
	tew rehst ahvehk mwah seht nwee?
I'd like to go to bed with you	**J'aimerais coucher avec toi**
	jhehmuhreh kooshay ahvehk twah
Only if we use a condom	**Seulement en utilisant un préservatif**
	suhlmohn ohn newteeleezohn uhn prayzehrvahteef
We have to be careful about AIDS	**Il faut être prudent à cause du sida**
	eel foa tehtr prewdohn ah koaz dew seedah
That's what they all say	**Ils disent tous pareil**
	eel deez toos pahrehy
We shouldn't take any risks	**Ne prenons aucun risque**
	nuh pruhnawn zoakuhn reesk
Do you have a condom?	**Tu as un préservatif?**
	tew ah zuhn prayzehrvahteef?
No? In that case we won't do it	**Non? Alors je ne veux pas**
	nawn? ahlor jhuh nuh vuh pah

3.11 Arrangements

When will I see you again?	**Quand est-ce que je te revois?**
	kohn tehs kuh jhuh tuh ruhvwah?
Are you free over the weekend?	**Vous êtes/tu es libre ce week-end?**
	voozeht/tew eh leebr suh week-ehnd?
What shall we arrange?	**Que décidons-nous?**
	kuh dayseedawn noo?
Where shall we meet?	**Où nous retrouvons-nous?**
	oo noo ruhtroovawn noo?
Will you pick me/us up?	**Vous venez me/nous chercher?**
	voo vuhnay muh/noo shehrshay?
Shall I pick you up?	**Je viens vous/te chercher?**
	jhuh vyahn voo/tuh shehrshay?

I have to be home by... _ **Je dois être à la maison à...heures**
jhuh dwah zehtr ah lah mehzawn ah...uhr

3.12 Saying goodbye

I don't want to see_____ **Je ne veux plus vous revoir**
 you anymore *jhuh nuh vuh plew voo ruhvwahr*

Can I take you home?__ **Puis-je vous raccompagner à la maison?**
*pwee jhuh voo rahkawnpahnyay ah lah
 mehzawn?*

Can I write/call you? ___ **Puis-je vous écrire/téléphoner?**
pwee jhuh voo zaykreer/taylayfonay?

Will you write/call me? _ **M'écrirez-vous/me téléphonerez-vous?**
maykreeray voo/muh taylayfonuhray voo?

Can I have your _____ **Puis-je avoir votre adresse/numéro de**
 address/phone **téléphone?**
 number? *pwee jhahvwahr votr ahdrehs/newmayroa
 duh taylayfon?*

Thanks for everything __ **Merci pour tout**
mehrsee poor too

It was very nice _____ **C'était très agréable**
sayteh treh zahgrayahbl

Say hello to... _____ **Présentez mes amitiés à...**
prayzohntay may zahmeetyay ah...

Good luck _____ **Bonne chance**
bon shohns

When will you be back? **Quand est-ce que tu reviens?**
kohn tehs kuh tew ruhvyahn?

I'll be waiting for you___ **Je t'attendrai**
jhuh tahtohndray

I'd like to see you again **J'aimerais te revoir**
jhehmuhreh tuh ruhvwahr

I hope we meet_____ again soon	**J'espère que nous nous reverrons bientôt** *jhehspehr kuh noo noo ruhvehrawn byahntoa*
You are welcome _____	**Vous êtes le/la bienvenu(e)** *voozeht luh/lah byahnvuhnew*

● **In France** people usually have three meals:

1 *Le petit déjeuner* (breakfast) approx. between 7.30 and 10am. Breakfast is light and consists of *café au lait* (white coffee) or lemon tea, a croissant, or slices of baguette (French bread), with butter and jam.

2 *Le déjeuner* (lunch) approx. between midday and 2pm. Lunch always includes a hot dish and is the most important meal of the day. Offices and shops often close and lunch is taken at home, in a restaurant or canteen (in some factories and schools). It usually consists of four courses:
– starter
– main course
– cheese
– dessert

3 *Le dîner* (dinner) between 7.30 and 9pm. Dinner is a light hot meal, usually taken with the family.

At around 5pm, a special snack (*le goûter*) is served to children, usually a roll or slices of baguette and biscuits with some chocolate.

4.1 On arrival

I'd like to book a table for seven o'clock, please?	**Puis-je réserver une table pour sept heures?** *pwee jhuh rayzehrvay ewn tahbl poor seht uhr?*
I'd like a table for two, please	**Une table pour deux personnes s'il vous plaît** *ewn tahbl poor duh pehrson seel voo pleh*
We've/we haven't booked	**Nous (n')avons (pas) réservé** *noo zahvawn/noo nahvawn pah rayzehrvay*
Is the restaurant open yet?	**Le restaurant est déjà ouvert?** *luh rehstoarohn eh dayjhah oovehr?*
What time does the restaurant open/close?	**A quelle heure ouvre/ferme le restaurant?** *ah kehl uhr oovr/fehrm luh rehstoarohn?*

Vous avez réservé?	Do you have a reservation?
A quel nom?	What name, please?
Par ici, s'il vous plaît.	This way, please
Cette table est réservée.	This table is reserved
Nous aurons une table de libre dans un quart d'heure.	We'll have a table free in fifteen minutes.
Voulez-vous patienter (au bar)?	Would you like to wait (at the bar)?

Can we wait for a_____ table?	Pouvons-nous attendre qu'une table soit libre?
	poovawn noo zahtohndr kewn tahbl swah leebr?
Do we have to wait ____ long?	Devons-nous attendre longtemps?
	devawn noo zahtohndr lawntohn?
Is this seat taken? _____	Est-ce que cette place est libre?
	ehs kuh seht plahs eh leebr?
Could we sit _____ here/there?	Pouvons-nous nous asseoir ici/là-bas?
	poovawn noo noo zahswahr eesee/lahbah?
Can we sit by the_____ window?	Pouvons-nous nous asseoir près de la fenêtre?
	poovawn noo noo zahswahr preh duh lah fuhnehtr?
Can we eat outside? ___	Pouvons-nous aussi manger dehors?
	poovawn noo zoasee mohnjhay duh-ohr?
Do you have another___ chair for us?	Avez-vous encore une chaise?
	ahvay voo zohnkor ewn shehz?
Do you have a _____ highchair?	Avez-vous une chaise haute?
	ahvay voo zewn shehz oat?
Is there a socket for____ this bottle-warmer?	Y a-t-il une prise pour ce chauffe-biberon?
	ee ya teel ewn preez poor suh shoaf beebuhrawn?

Could you warm up this bottle/jar for me?	Pouvez-vous me réchauffer ce biberon/ce petit pot?
	poovay voo muh rayshoafay suh beebuhrawn/suh puhtee poa?
Not too hot, please	Pas trop chaud s'il vous plaît
	pah troa shoa seel voo pleh
Is there somewhere I can change the baby's nappy?	Y a-t-il ici une pièce où je peux m'occuper du bébé?
	ee ya teel eesee ewn pyehs oo jhuh puh mokewpay dew baybay?
Where are the toilets?	Où sont les toilettes?
	oo sawn lay twahleht?

4.2 Ordering

Waiter!	Garçon!
	gahrsawn!
Madam!	Madame!
	mahdahm!
Sir!	Monsieur!
	muhsyuh!
We'd like something to eat/a drink	Nous aimerions manger/boire quelque chose
	noo zaymuhryawn mohnjhay/bwahr kehlkuh shoaz
Could I have a quick meal?	Puis-je rapidement manger quelque chose?
	pwee jhuh rahpeedmohn mohnjhay kehlkuh shoaz?
We don't have much time	Nous avons peu de temps
	noo zavawn puh duh tohn
We'd like to have a drink first	Nous voulons d'abord boire quelque chose
	noo voolawn dahbor bwahr kehlkuh shoaz

Could we see the _____ menu/wine list, please?	**Pouvons-nous avoir la carte/la carte des vins?** *poovawn noo zahvwahr lah kahrt/lah kahrt day vahn?*
Do you have a menu ___ in English?	**Vous avez un menu en anglais?** *voo zahvay zuhn muhnew ohn nohngleh?*
Do you have a dish ____ of the day?	**Vous avez un plat du jour?** *voo zahvay zuhn plah dew jhoor?*
We haven't made a ____ choice yet	**Nous n'avons pas encore choisi** *noo nahvawn pah zohnkor shwahzee*
What do you _____ recommend?	**Qu'est-ce que vous nous conseillez?** *kehs kuh voo noo kawnsayay?*
What are the _____ specialities of the region/the house?	**Quelles sont les spécialités de cette région/de la maison?** *kehl sawn lay spaysyahleetay duh seht rayjhyawn/duh lah mehzawn?*
I like strawberries/ _____ olives	**J'aime les fraises/les olives** *jhehm lay frehz/lay zoleev*
I don't like meat/fish/... _	**Je n'aime pas la viande/le poisson/...** *jhuh nehm pah lah vyohnd/luh pwahssawn/...*
What's this? _____	**Qu'est-ce que c'est?** *kehs kuh seh?*

Vous désirez prendre un apéritif?	Would you like a drink first?
Vous avez déjà fait votre choix?	Have you decided?
Que désirez-vous boire?	What would you like to drink?
Bon appétit	Enjoy your meal
Vous désirez votre viande saignante, à point ou bien cuite?	Would you like your steak rare, medium or well done?
Vous désirez un dessert/du café?	Would you like a dessert/coffee?

Does it have...in it? ___	Y a-t-il du/de la/des...dedans?
	ee ya teel dew/duh lah/day...duhdohn?
What does it taste ___ like?	A quoi cela ressemble-t-il?
	ah kwah suhlah ruhsohnbluh teel?
Is this a hot or a _____ cold dish?	Ce plat, est-il chaud ou froid?
	suh plah, eh teel shoa oo frwah?
Is this sweet? _____	Ce plat, est-il sucré?
	suh plah, eh teel sewkray?
Is this spicy? _____	Ce plat, est-il épicé?
	suh plah, eh teel aypeesay?
Do you have anything __ else, please?	Vous avez peut-être autre chose?
	voo zahvay puh tehtr oatr shoaz?
I'm on a salt-free diet __	Le sel m'est interdit
	luh sehl meh tahntehrdee
I can't eat pork _____	La viande de porc m'est interdite
	lah vyohnd duh por meh tahntehrdeet
– sugar _____	Le sucre m'est interdit
	luh sewkr meh tahntehrdee
– fatty foods _____	Le gras m'est interdit
	luh grah meh tahntehrdee
– (hot) spices_____	Les épices (fortes) me sont interdites
	lay zaypees (fort) muh sawn tahntehrdeet
I'll have what those ___ people are having	J'aimerais la même chose que ces personnes-là
	jhehmuhreh lah mehm shoaz kuh say pehrson lah
I'd like... _____	J'aimerais...
	jhehmuhreh...
We're not having a_____ starter	Nous ne prenons pas d'entrée
	noo nuh pruhnawn pah dohntray
The child will share ___ what we're having	L'enfant partagera notre menu
	lohnfohn pahrtahjhuhrah notr muhnew
Could I have some_____ more bread, please?	Encore du pain s'il vous plaît
	ohnkor dew pahn seel voo pleh
– a bottle of water/ ___ wine	Une autre bouteille d'eau/de vin
	ewn oatr bootehy doa/duh vahn

– another helping of...	**Une autre portion de...**
	ewn oatr porsyawn duh...
– some salt and pepper	**Pouvez-vous apporter du sel et du poivre?**
	poovay voo zahportay dew sehl ay dew pwahvr?
– a napkin	**Pouvez-vous apporter une serviette?**
	poovay voo zahportay ewn sehrvyeht?
– a spoon	**Pouvez-vous apporter une cuillère?**
	poovay voo zahportay ewn kweeyehr?
– an ashtray	**Pouvez-vous apporter un cendrier?**
	poovay voo zahportay uhn sohndryay?
– some matches	**Pouvez-vous apporter des allumettes?**
	poovay voo zahportay day zahlewmeht?
– some toothpicks	**Pouvez-vous apporter des cure-dents?**
	poovay voo zahportay day kewr dohn?
– a glass of water	**Pouvez-vous apporter un verre d'eau?**
	poovay voo zahportay uhn vehr doa?
– a straw (for the child)	**Pouvez-vous apporter une paille (pour l'enfant)?**
	poovay voo zahportay ewn paheey (poor lohnfohn)?
Enjoy your meal!	**Bon appétit!**
	bohn nahpaytee!
You too!	**De même vous aussi**
	duh mehm voo zoasee
Cheers!	**Santé!**
	sohntay!
The next round's on me	**La prochaine tournée est pour moi**
	lah proshehn toornay eh poor mwah
Could we have a doggy bag, please?	**Pouvons-nous emporter les restes pour notre chien?**
	poovawn noo zohnportay lay rehst poor notr shyahn?

4.3 The bill

See also 8.2 Settling the bill

How much is this _____ dish?	**Quel est le prix de ce plat?** *kehl eh luh pree duh suh plah?*
Could I have the bill, ___ please?	**L'addition s'il vous plaît** *lahdeesyawn seel voo pleh*
All together _____	**Tout ensemble** *too tohnsohnbl*
Everyone pays _____ separately	**Chacun paye pour soi** *shahkuhn pehy poor swah*
Could we have the ___ menu again, please?	**Pouvons-nous revoir la carte?** *poovawn noo ruhvwahr lah kahrt?*
The...is not on the bill _	**Le...n'est pas sur l'addition** *luh...neh pah sewr lahdeesyawn*

4.4 Complaints

It's taking a very _____ long time	**C'est bien long** *seh byahn lawn*
We've been here an____ hour already.	**Nous sommes ici depuis une heure** *noo som zeesee duhpwee zewn uhr*
This must be a mistake_	**Cela doit être une erreur** *suhlah dwah tehtr ewn ehruhr*
This is not what I _____ ordered.	**Ce n'est pas ce que j'ai commandé** *suh neh pah suh kuh jhay komohnday*
I ordered..._____	**J'ai commandé un...** *jhay komohnday uhn...*
There's a dish missing__	**Il manque un plat** *eel mohnk uhn plah*
This is broken/ _____ not clean	**C'est cassé/ce n'est pas propre** *seh kahssay/suh neh pah propr*
The food's cold_____	**Le plat est froid** *luh plah eh frwah*

– not fresh _____	**Le plat n'est pas frais** *luh plah neh pah freh*
– too salty/sweet/spicy _	**Le plat est trop salé/sucré/épicé** *luh plah eh troa sahlay/sewkray/aypeesay*
The meat's not done ___	**La viande n'est pas cuite** *lah vyohnd neh pah kweet*
– overdone _____	**La viande est trop cuite** *lah vyohnd eh troa kweet*
– tough_____	**La viande est dure** *lah vyohnd eh dewr*
– off_____	**La viande est avariée** *lah vyohnd eh tahvahryay*
Could I have _____ something else instead of this?	**Vous pouvez me donner autre chose à la place?** *voo poovay muh donay oatr shoaz ah lah plahs?*
The bill/this amount is _ not right	**L'addition/cette somme n'est pas exacte** *lahdeesyawn/seht som neh pah zehgzahkt*
We didn't have this ____	**Ceci nous ne l'avons pas eu** *suhsee noo nuh lahvawn pah zew*
There's no paper in the _ toilet	**Il n'y a plus de papier hygiénique dans les toilettes** *eel nee yah plew duh pahpyay eejhyayneek dohn lay twahleht*
Do you have a _____ complaints book?	**Avez-vous un registre de réclamations?** *ahvay voo zuhn ruhjheestr duh rayklahmahsyawn?*
Will you call the _____ manager, please?	**Voulez-vous appeler le directeur s'il vous plaît?** *voolay voo zahpuhlay luh deerehktuhr seel voo pleh?*

4.5 Paying a compliment

That was a wonderful __ **Nous avons très bien mangé**
meal *noo zahvawn treh byahn mohnjhay*

The food was excellent_ **Le repas était succulent**
luh ruhpah ayteh sewkewlohn

The...in particular was__ **Le...surtout était délicieux**
delicious *luh...sewrtoo ayteh dayleesyuh*

4.6 The menu

apéritifs	**gibier**	**plat principal**
aperitifs	game	main course
boissons alcoolisées	**hors d'oeuvres**	**potages**
alcoholic beverages	starters	soups
boissons chaudes	**légumes**	**service compris**
hot beverages	vegetables	service included
carte des vins	**plats chauds**	**spécialités**
wine list	hot dishes	**régionales**
coquillages	**plats froids**	regional specialities
shellfish	cold dishes	**viandes**
desserts	**plat du jour**	meat dishes
sweets	dish of the day	**volailles**
fromages	**pâtisserie**	poultry
cheese	pastry	

4.7 Alphabetical list of drinks and dishes

agneau lamb	**biscuit** biscuit	**champignons** mushrooms
ail garlic	**boeuf** beef	**crème chantilly** cream (whipped)
amandes almonds	**boissons alcoolisées** alcoholic beverages	**châtaigne** chestnut
ananas pineapple	**boissons chaudes/ froides** hot/cold beverages	**chausson aux pommes** apple turnover
anchois anchovy	**boudin noir/blanc** black/white pudding	**chou-fleur** cauliflower
anguille eel	**brochet** pike	**choucroute** sauerkraut
anis aniseed	**cabillaud** cod	**chou** cabbage
apéritif aperitif	**café (noir/au lait)** coffee (black/white)	**choux de Bruxelles** Brussels sprouts
artichaut artichoke	**caille** quail	**citron** lemon
asperge asparagus	**calmar** squid	**civet de lièvre** jugged hare
baguette french stick	**canard** duck	**clou de girofle** clove
banane banana	**câpres** capers	**cocktails** cocktails
beurre butter	**carpe** carp	**cognac** brandy
biftec steak	**carte des vins** wine list	**concombre** cucumber
bière (bière pression) beer (draught beer)	**céleri** celery	**confiture** jam
	cerises cherries	**consommé** broth

coquillages shellfish	**cru** raw	**épinards** spinach
coquilles Saint-Jacques scallops	**crustacés** seafood	**escargots** snails
cornichon gherkin	**cuisses de grenouilles** frog's legs	**farine** flour
côte/côtelette chop	**cuit(à l'eau)** boiled	**fenouil** fennel
côte de boeuf T-bone steak	**dattes** dates	**fèves** broad beans
côte de porc pork chop	**daurade** sea bream	**figues** figs
côtelette d'agneau lamb chop	**dessert** sweet	**filet de boeuf** fillet
côtelettes dans l'échine spare rib	**eau minérale gazeuse/non gazeuse** sparkling/still mineral water	**filet mignon** fillet steak
couvert cutlery	**échalote** shallot	**filet de porc** tenderloin
crabe crab	**écrevisse** crayfish	**fines herbes** herbs
crêpes pancakes	**endives** chicory	**foie gras** goose liver
crevettes grises shrimps	**entrecôte** sirloin steak	**fraises** strawberries
crevettes roses prawns	**entrées** first course	**framboises** raspberries
croissant croissant	**épices** spices	**frit** fried
croque monsieur toasted ham and cheese sandwich		**friture** deep-fried
		fromage cheese

fruit de la passion
passion fruit

fruits de la saison
seasonal fruits

gaufres
waffles

gigot d'agneau
leg of lamb

glace
ice cream

glaçons
ice cubes

grillé
grilled

groseilles
redcurrants

hareng
herring

haricots blancs
haricot beans

haricots verts
french beans

homard
lobster

hors d'oeuvre
starters

huîtres
oysters

jambon blanc/cru/fumé
ham(cooked/Parma style)/smoked)

jus de citron
lemon juice

jus de fruits
fruit juice

jus d'orange
orange juice

lait/demi-écrémé/ entier
milk/semi-skimmed/ full-cream

langouste
crayfish

langoustine
scampi

langue
tongue

lapin
rabbit

légumes
vegetables

lentilles
lentils

liqueur
liqueur

lotte
monkfish

loup de mer
sea bass

macaron
macaroon

maïs
sweetcorn

épis de maïs
corn (on the cob)

marron
chestnut

melon
melon

menu du jour/à la carte
menu of the day/à la carte

morilles
morels

moules
mussels

mousse au chocolat
chocolate mousse

moutarde
mustard

myrtilles
bilberries

noisette
hazelnut

noix
walnut

noix de veau
fillet of veal

oeuf à la coque/dur/au plat
egg soft/hard boiled/fried

oignon
onion

olives
olives

omelette
omelette

origan
oregano

pain au chocolat
chocolate bun

part
portion

pastis	pommes de terre	service compris/non compris
pastis	potatoes	service (not) included
pâtisserie	pommes frites	sole
pastry	chips	sole
pêche	poulet(blanc)	soupe
peach	chicken(breast)	soup
petite friture	prune	soupe à l'oignon
fried fish(whitebait or similar)	plum	onion soup
petits (biscuits) salés	pruneaux	spécialités régionales
savoury biscuits	prunes	regional specialities
petit pain	queue de boeuf	sucre
roll	oxtail	sugar
petits pois	ragoût	thon
green peas	stew	tuna
pigeon	ris de veau	thym
pigeon	sweetbread	thyme
pintade	riz	tripes
guinea fowl	rice	tripe
plat du jour	rôti de boeuf (rosbif)	truffes
dish of the day	roast beef	truffles
plats froids/chauds	rouget	truite
cold/hot courses	red mullet	trout
poire	saignant	truite saumonée
pear	rare	salmon trout
pois chiches	salade verte	turbot
chick peas	lettuce	turbot
poisson	salé/sucré	vapeur (à la)
fish	salted/sweet	steamed
poivre	sandwich	venaison
pepper	sandwich	venison
poivron	saumon	viande hachée
green/red pepper	salmon	minced meat/mince
pomme	sel	vin blanc
apple	salt	white wine

vin rosé	**vinaigre**
rosé wine	vinegar
vin rouge	**xérès**
red wine	sherry

5 On the road

5.1 Asking for directions

Excuse me, could I ask you something?	**Pardon, puis-je vous demander quelque chose?**
	pahrdawn, pwee jhuh voo duhmohnday kehlkuh shoaz?
I've lost my way _____	**Je me suis égaré(e)**
	jhuh muh swee zaygahray
Is there an... around here?	**Connaissez-vous un...dans les environs?**
	konehssay voo zuhn... dohn lay zohnveerawn?
Is this the way to...? ___	**Est-ce la route vers...?**
	ehs lah root vehr...?
Could you tell me how to get to...?	**Pouvez-vous me dire comment aller à...?**
	poovay voo muh deer komohn tahlay ah...?
What's the quickest way to...?	**Comment puis-je arriver le plus vite possible à...?**
	komohn pwee jhuh ahreevay luh plew veet pohseebl ah...?
How many kilometres is it to...?	**Il y a encore combien de kilomètres jusqu'à...?**
	eel ee yah ohnkor kohnbyahn duh keeloamehtr jhewskah...?

Je ne sais pas, je ne suis pas d'ici	I don't know, I don't know my way around here
Vous vous êtes trompé	You're going the wrong way
Vous devez retourner à... Là-bas les panneaux vous indiqueront la route	You have to go back to... From there on just follow the signs
Là-bas vous demanderez à nouveau votre route	When you get there, ask again

Could you point it out on the map?	Pouvez-vous me l'indiquer sur la carte? *poovay voo muh lahndeekay sewr lah kahrt?*

tout droit straight ahead	le feu (de signalisation) the traffic light	le pont the bridge
à gauche left	le tunnel the tunnel	le passage à niveau the level crossing
à droite right	le panneau `cédez la priorité' the `give way' sign	la barrière boom
tourner turn	l'immeuble the building	le panneau direction... the sign pointing to...
suivre follow	à l'angle, au coin at the corner	la flèche the arrow
traverser cross	la rivière, le fleuve the river	
le carrefour the intersection	l'autopont the fly-over	
la rue the street		

5.2 Customs

● **Border documents** along with your passport you must carry your original documents with you. These include your valid full driving licence (together with paper counterpart if photocard licence), vehicle registration document and motor insurance certificate. Contact your motor insurer for advice at least a month before taking your vehicle overseas to ensure that you are adequately covered. It is advisable to carry a fire extinguisher, first-aid kit and warning triangle. Entry regulations can change at very short notice, so you are advised to check with your travel agent, airline, ferry or rail company that you have the correct documentation before your journey.

Votre passeport s'il vous plaît	Your passport, please
La carte verte s'il vous plaît	Your green card, please
La carte grise s'il vous plaît	Your vehicle documents, please
Votre visa s'il vous plaît	Your visa, please
Où allez-vous?	Where are you heading?
Combien de temps pensez-vous rester?	How long are you planning to stay?
Avez-vous quelque chose à déclarer?	Do you have anything to declare?
Voulez-vous l'ouvrir?	Open this, please

My children are _____ entered on this passport	Mes enfants sont inscrits dans ce passeport
	may zohnfohn sawn tahnskree dohn suh pahspor
I'm travelling through___	Je suis de passage
	jhuh swee duh pahsahjh
I'm going on holiday ___ to...	Je vais en vacances en...
	jhuh veh zohn vahkohns ohn...
I'm on a business trip ___	Je suis en voyage d'affaires
	jhuh swee zohn vwahyahjh dahfehr
I don't know how _____ long I'll be staying yet	Je ne sais pas encore combien de temps je reste
	jhuh nuh seh pah zohnkor kawnbyahn duh tohn jhuh rehst
I'll be staying here for __ a weekend	Je reste un week-end ici
	jhuh rehst uhn weekehnd eesee
– for a few days _____	Je reste quelques jours ici
	jhuh rehst kehlkuh jhoor eesee
– for a week _____	Je reste une semaine ici
	jhuh rehst ewn suhmehn eesee
–for two weeks _____	Je reste quinze jours ici
	jhuh rehst kahnz jhoor eesee

I've got nothing to _____ declare	Je n'ai rien à déclarer *jhuh nay ryahn nah dayklahray*
I've got...with me _____	J'ai... avec moi *jhay... ahvehk mwah*
– ...cartons of _____ cigarettes	J'ai des cartouches de cigarettes *jhay day kahrtoosh duh seegahreht*
– ...bottles of... _____	J'ai des bouteilles de... *jhay day bootehy duh...*
– some souvenirs_____	J'ai quelques souvenirs *jhay kehlkuh soovneer*
These are personal _____ effects	Ce sont des affaires personnelles *suh sawn day zahfehr pehrsonehl*
These are not new _____	Ces affaires ne sont pas neuves *say zahfehr nuh sawn pah nuhv*
Here's the receipt_____	Voici la facture *vwahsee lah fahktewr*
This is for private use __	C'est pour usage personnel *seh poor ewzahjh pehrsonehl*
How much import duty _ do I have to pay?	Combien de droits d'importation dois-je payer? *kawnbyahn duh drwah dahnpohrtasyawn dwah jhuh payay?*
Can I go now? _____	Puis-je partir maintenant? *pwee jhuh pahrteer mahntuhnohn?*

5.3 Luggage

Porter! _____	Porteur! *portuhr!*
Could you take this _____ luggage to...?	Voulez-vous porter ces bagages à... s'il vous plaît? *voolay voo portay say bahgahjh ah... seel voo pleh?*
How much do I_____ owe you?	Combien vous dois-je? *kawnbyahn voo dwah jhuh?*

Where can I find a ____ luggage trolley?	Où puis-je trouver un chariot pour les bagages?	
	oo pwee jhuh troovay uhn shahryoa poor lay bahgahjh?	
Could you store this ___ luggage for me?	Puis-je mettre ces bagages en consigne?	
	pwee jhuh mehtr say bahgahjh ohn kawnseenyuh?	
Where are the luggage _ lockers?	Où est la consigne automatique?	
	oo eh lah kawnseenyuh oatoamahteek?	
I can't get the locker ____ open	Je n'arrive pas à ouvrir la consigne	
	jhuh nahreev pah zah oovreer lah kawnseenyuh	
How much is it _____ per item per day?	Combien cela coûte-t-il par bagage par jour?	
	kawnbyahn suhlah koot-uh teel pahr bahgahjh pahr jhoor?	
This is not my bag/ ____ suitcase	Ce n'est pas mon sac/ma valise	
	suh neh pah mawn sahk/mah vahleez	
There's one item/bag/ __ suitcase missing still	Il manque encore une chose/un sac/une valise	
	eel mohnk ohnkor ewn shoaz/uhn sahk/ewn vahleez	
My suitcase is_____ damaged	Ma valise est abîmée	
	mah vahleez eh tahbeemay	

5.4 Traffic signs

accès interdit à tous les véhicules	allumez vos feux	bison fûté
no entry	switch on lights	recommended route
accotement non stabilisé	autoroute	brouillard fréquent
soft verge	motorway	beware fog
	barrière de dégel	cédez le passage
	road closed	give way

chaussée à gravillons
loose chippings

chaussée déformée
uneven road surface

chaussée glissante
slippery road

circulation alternée
alternate priority

danger
danger

carrefour dangereux
dangerous crossing

danger priorité à droite
priority to vehicles from right

descente dangereuse
steep hill

déviation
diversion

fin de...
end of...

fin d'allumage des feux
end of need for lights

fin de chantier
end of road works

interdiction de dépasser
no overtaking

interdiction de klaxonner
no horns

interdiction sauf riverains
access only

limite de vitesse
speed limit

passage à niveau
level crossing

passage d'animaux
animals crossing

passage pour piétons
pedestrian crossing

péage
toll

poids lourds
heavy goods vehicles

rappel
reminder

remorques et semi-remorques
lorries and articulated lorries

sens unique
one-way traffic

serrez à droite
keep right

sortie
exit

sortie de camions
factory/works exit

interdiction de stationner
no parking

taxis
taxi rank

travaux (sur...km)
roadworks ahead

véhicules lents
slow traffic

véhicules transportant des matières dangereuses
vehicles transporting dangerous substances

verglas fréquent
ice on road

virages sur...km
bends for...km

vitesse limite
maximum speed

zone bleue
parking disc required

zone piétonne
pedestrian zone

5.5 The car

● Particular traffic regulations:
–maximum speed for cars:
130km/h on toll roads, 110km/h in wet weather
110km/h on other motorways, 100km/h in wet weather
90km/h outside built-up areas, 80km/h in wet weather
50km/h in built-up areas
It is recommended that all vehicles used dipped headlights day and
night outside built-up areas.

5.6 The petrol station

● **Petrol is equally expensive** in France although diesel can be
cheaper.

How many kilometres __ to the next petrol station, please?	Il y a combien de kilomètres jusqu'à la prochaine station-service? *eel ee yah kawnbyahn duh keeloamehtr jhewskah lah proshehn stasyawn sehrvees?*
I would like...litres of..., _ please	Je voudrais ... litres *jhuh voodreh ... leetr*
– 4-star_____	Je voudrais ... litres de super *jhuh voodreh ... leetr duh sewpehr*
– leaded _____	Je voudrais ... litres d'essence ordinaire *jhuh voodreh ... leetr dehssohns ohrdeenehr*
– unleaded_____	Je voudrais ... litres d'essence sans plomb *jhuh voodreh ... leetr dehssohns sohn plawn*

– diesel	Je voudrais ... litres de gazoil
	jhuh voodreh ... leetr duh gahzwahl
I would like...francs worth of petrol, please.	Je voudrais pour ... francs d'essence s'il vous plaît
	jhuh voodreh poor ... frohn dehssohns seel voo pleh
Fill it up, please	Le plein s'il vous plaît
	luh plahn seel voo pleh
Could you check...?	Vous voulez contrôler...?
	voo voolay kawntroalay...?
– the oil level	Vous voulez contrôler le niveau d'huile?
	voo voolay kawntroalay luh neevoa dweel?
– the tyre pressure	Vous voulez contrôler la pression des pneus?
	voo voolay kawntroalay lah prehsyawn day pnuh?
Could you change the oil, please?	Vous pouvez changer l'huile?
	voo poovay shohnjhay lweel?
Could you clean the windows/the windscreen, please?	Vous pouvez nettoyer les vitres/le pare-brise?
	voo poovay nehtwahyay lay veetr/luh pahrbreez?
Could you give the car a wash, please?	Vous pouvez faire laver la voiture?
	voo poovay fehr lahvay lah vwahtewr?

The parts of a car

battery	la batterie	*lah bahtree*
rear light	le feu arrière	*luh fuh ahryehr*
rear-view mirror	le rétroviseur	*luh raytroaveezuhr*
reversing light	le phare de recul	*luh fahr duh ruhkewl*
aerial	l'antenne(f.)	*lohntehn*
car radio	l'autoradio(m.)	*loatoarahdyoa*
petrol tank	le réservoir d'essence	*luh rayzehrvwahr dehssohns*
inside mirror	le rétroviseur intérieur	*luh raytroaveezuhr ahntayryuhr*
sparking plugs	les bougies(f.)	*llay boojhee*
fuel filter/pump	le filtre à carburant	*luh feeltr ah kahrbewrohn*
	la pompe à carburant	*lah pawnp ah kahrbewrohn*
wing mirror	le rétroviseur de côté	*luh raytroaveezuhr duh koatay*
bumper	le pare-chocs	*luh pahr shok*
carburettor	le carburateur	*luh kahrbewrahtuhr*
crankcase	le carter	*lluh kahrtehr*
cylinder	le cylindre	*luh seelahndr*
ignition	l'allumage	*l'ahlewmahjh*
warning light	la lampe témoin	*lah lohnp taymwahn*
dynamo	la dynamo	*lah deenahmoa*
accelerator	l'accélérateur	*lahksaylayrahtuhr*
handbrake	le frein à main	*luh frahn ah mahn*
valve	la soupape	*lah soopahp*
silencer	le silencieux	*luh seelohnsyuh*
boot	le coffre	*luh kofr*
headlight	le phare	*luh fahr*
crank shaft	le vilebrequin	*luh veelbruhkahn*
air filter	le filtre à air	*luh feeltr ah ehr*
fog lamp	le phare anti-brouillar	*luh fahr ohntee brooy-yahr*

engine block	le bloc moteur	*luh blok motuhr*
camshaft	l'arbre à cames	*lahrbr ah kahm*
oil filter/pump	le filtre à huile	*luh feeltr ah weel*
	la pompe à huile	*lah pawnp ah weel*
dipstick	la jauge du niveau d'huile	*lah jhoajh dew neevoa dweel*
pedal	la pédale	*lah paydahl*
door	la portière	*lah portyehr*
radiator	le radiateur	*luh rahdyahtuhr*
disc brake	le frein à disque	*luh frahn ah deesk*
spare wheel	la roue de secours	*lah roo duh suhkoor*
indicator	le clignotant	*luh kleenyohtohn*
windscreen wiper	l'essuie-glace(m.)	*lehswee glahs*
shock absorbers	les amortisseurs(m.)	*lay zahmorteesuhr*
sunroof	le toit ouvrant	*luh twah oovrohn*
starter motor	le démarreur	*luh daymahruhr*
steering column	la colonne de direction	*lah kolon duh deerehksyawn*
steering wheel	le volant	*luh volohn*
exhaust pipe	le tuyau d'échappement	*luh tweeyoa dayshahpmohn*
seat belt	la ceinture de sécurité	*lah sahntewr duh saykewreetay*
fan	le ventilateur	*luh vohnteelahtuhr*
distributor cable	le câble distributeur	*luh kahbl deestreebewtuhr*
gear lever	le levier de vitesses	*luh luhvyay duh veetehs*
windscreen	le pare-brise	*luh pahrbreez*
water pump	la pompe à eau	*lah pawnp ah oa*
wheel	la roue	*lah roo*
hubcap	l'enjoliveur	*lohnjholeevuhr*
piston	le piston	*luh peestawn*

The parts of a bicycle

rear lamp	le feu arrière	*luh fuh ahryehr*
rear wheel	la roue arrière	*lah roo ahryehr*
(luggage) carrier	le porte-bagages	*luh port bahgahjh*
bicycle fork	la tête de fourche	*lah teht duh foorsh*
bell	la sonnette	*lah sohneht*
inner tube	la chambre à air	*lah shohnbr ah ehr*
tyre	le pneu	*luh pnuh*
crank	le pédalier	*luh paydahlyay*
gear change	le changement de vitesse	*luh shohnjhmohn duh veetehs*
wire	le fil (électrique)	*luh feel (aylehktreek)*
dynamo	la dynamo	*lah deenahmoa*
bicycle trailer	la remorque de bicyclette	*lah ruhmork duh beeseekleht*
frame	le cadre	*luh kahdr*
dress guard	le protège-jupe	*luh protehjh jhewp*
chain	la chaîne	*lah shehn*
chainguard	le carter	*luh kahrtehr*
padlock	l'antivol(m.)	*lohnteevol*
milometer	le compteur kilométrique	*luh kawntuhr keeloamaytreek*
child's seat	le siège-enfant	*luh syehjh ohnfohn*
headlamp	le phare	*luh fahr*
bulb	l'ampoule(f.)	*lohnpool*
pedal	la pédale	*lah paydahl*
pump	la pompe	*lah pawnp*
reflector	le réflecteur	*luh rayflehktuhr*
break blocks	les patins	*lay pahtahn*
brake cable	le câble de frein	*luh kahbl duh frahn*
wheel lock	le cadenas pour bicyclette	*lah kaduhnah poor beeseekleht*
carrier straps	le tendeur	*luh tohnduhr*

tachometer	le compteur de vitesse	*luh kawntuhr duh veetehs*
spoke	le rayon	*luh rayawn*
mudguard	le garde-boue	*luh gahrd boo*
handlebar	le guidon	*luh gueedawn*
chain wheel	le pignon	*luh peenyawn*
toe clip	le câle-pied	*luh kahl pyay*
crank axle	l'axe du pédalier(m.)	*lahx dew paydahlyay*
drum brake	le frein à tambour	*luh frahn ah tohnboor*
rim	la jante	*lah jhohnt*
valve	la valve	*lah vahlv*
valve tube	le raccord souple de la valve	*luh rahkor soopl duh lah vahlv*
gear cable	la chaîne du dérailleur	*lah shehn dew dayrahyuhr*
fork	la fourche	*lah foorsh*
front wheel	la roue avant	*lah roo ahvohn*
saddle	la selle	*lah sehl*

5.7 Breakdown and repairs

I'm having car trouble.
Could you give me a
hand?
Je suis en panne. Vous pouvez m'aider?
jhuh swee zohn pahnn. voo poovay mayday?

I've run out of petrol
Je n'ai plus d'essence
jhuh neh plew dehssohns

I've locked the keys
in the car
J'ai laissé les clefs dans la voiture fermée
jhay layssay lay klay dohn lah vwahtewr fehrmay

The car/motorbike/
moped won't start
La voiture/la moto/le vélomoteur ne démarre pas
lah vwahtewr/lah moatoa/luh vayloamotuhr nuh daymahr pah

Could you contact the
recovery service for
me, please?
Vous pouvez m'appeler l'assistance routière?
voo poovay mahpuhlay lahseestohns rootyehr?

Could you call a
garage for me, please?
Vous pouvez m'appeler un garage?
voo poovay mahpuhlay uhn gahrahjh?

Could you give me
a lift to...?
Puis-je aller avec vous jusqu'à ...?
pwee jhahlay ahvehk voo jhewskah ...?

– a garage/into town?
Puis-je aller avec vous jusqu'à un garage/la ville?
pwee jhahlay ahvehk voo jhewskah uhn gahrahjh/lah veel?

– a phone booth?
Puis-je aller avec vous jusqu'à une cabine téléphonique?
pwee jhahlay ahvehk voo jhewskah ewn kahbeen taylayfoneek?

– an emergency
phone?
Puis-je aller avec vous jusqu'à un téléphone d'urgence?
pwee jhalay ahvehk voo jhewskah uhn taylayfon dewrjhohns?

Can we take my _____ bicycle/moped?	Est-ce que vous pouvez également prendre mon vélo(moteur)?
	ehs kuh voo poovay aygahlmohn prohndr mawn vayloa(motuhr)?
Could you tow me to___ a garage?	Vous pouvez me remorquer jusqu'à un garage?
	voo poovay muh ruhmorkay jhewskah uhn gahrahjh?
There's probably_____ something wrong with...(See pages 72–73)	Le ... a certainement quelque chose de défectueux
	luh ... ah sehrtehnemohn kehlkuh shoaz duh dayfehktewuh
Can you fix it? _____	Vous pouvez le réparer?
	voo poovay luh raypahray?
Could you fix my tyre? _	Vous pouvez réparer mon pneu?
	voo poovay raypahray mawn pnuh?
Could you change this _ wheel?	Vous pouvez changer cette roue?
	voo poovay shohnjhay seht roo?
Can you fix it so it'll____ get me to...?	Vous pouvez le réparer pour que je puisse rouler jusqu'à...?
	voo poovay luh raypahray poor kuh jhuh pwees roolay jhewskah...?
Which garage can _____ help me?	Quel garage pourrait m'aider?
	kehl gahrahjh pooreh mayday?
When will my_____ car/bicycle be ready?	Quand est-ce que ma voiture/ma bicyclette sera prête?
	kohn tehs kuh mah vwahtewr/mah beeseeklehtt suhrah preht?
Can I wait for it here? __	Je peux l'attendre ici?
	jhuh puh lahtohndr eesee?
How much will it cost? _	Combien cela va coûter?
	kawnbyahn suhlah vah kootay?
Could you itemise _____ the bill?	Vous pouvez me détailler la note?
	voo poovay muh daytahyay lah not?

Can I have a receipt ___   Puis-je avoir un reçu pour l'assurance?
for the insurance?   *pwee jhahvwahr uhn ruhsew poor*
                      lahsewrohns?

5.8 The bicycle/moped

● **Cycle paths** are rare in France. Bikes can be hired at tourist
centres (*vélo tout terrain* = mountain bike). Not much consideration
for bikes should be expected on the roads. The maximum speed for
mopeds is 45km/h both inside and outside town centres. A helmet is
compulsory.

Je n'ai pas les pièces détachées pour votre voiture/bicyclette	I don't have parts for your car/bicycle
Je dois aller chercher les pièces détachées ailleurs	I have to get the parts from somewhere else
Je dois commander les pièces détachées	I have to order the parts
Cela prendra une demi-journée	That'll take half a day
Cela prendra une journée	That'll take a day
Cela prendra quelques jours	That'll take a few days
Cela prendra une semaine	That'll take a week
Votre voiture est bonne pour la ferraille	Your car is a write-off
Il n'y a plus rien à y faire	It can't be repaired.
La voiture/la moto/la mobylette/la bicyclette sera prête à... heures	The car/motor bike/moped/bicycle will be ready at... o'clock.

5.9 Renting a vehicle

I'd like to rent a... _____	J'aimerais louer un... *jhehmuhreh looay uhn...*
Do I need a (special) _____ licence for that?	Me faut-il un permis spécial? *muh foa teel uhn pehrmee spaysyal?*
I'd like to rent the... _____ for...	Je voudrais louer le/la...pour *jhuh voodreh looay luh/lah...poor*
– one day _____	Je voudrais louer le/la...pour une journée *jhuh voodreh looay luh/lah...poor ewn jhoornay*
– two days _____	Je voodreh louer le/la...pour deux jours *jhuh voodreh looay luh/lah...poor duh jhoor*
How much is that per _____ day/week?	C'est combien par jour/semaine? *seh kawnbyahn pahr jhoor/suhmehn?*
How much is the _____ deposit?	De combien est la caution? *duh kawnbyahn eh lah koasyawn?*
Could I have a receipt _____ for the deposit?	Puis-je avoir un reçu pour la caution? *pwee jhahvwahr uhn ruhsew poor lah koasyawn?*
How much is the _____ surcharge per kilometre?	Quel est le supplément par kilomètre? *kehl eh luh sewplaymohn pahr keeloamehtr?*
Does that include _____ petrol?	Est-ce que l'essence est incluse? *ehs kuh lehsohns eh tahnklewz?*
Does that include _____ insurance?	Est-ce que l'assurance est incluse? *ehs kuh lahsewrohns eh tahnklewz?*
What time can I pick _____ the...up tomorrow?	Demain, à quelle heure puis-je venir chercher la...? *duhmahn ah kehl uhr pwee jhuh vuhneer shehrshay lah...?*
When does the...have _____ to be back?	Quand dois-je rapporter la...? *kohn dwah jhuh rahportay lah...?*

Where's the petrol tank?	Où est le réservoir?
	oo eh luh rayzehrvwahr?
What sort of fuel does it take?	Quel carburant faut-il utiliser?
	kehl kahrbewrohn foa teel ewteeleezay?

5.10 Hitchhiking

Where are you heading?	Où allez-vous?
	oo ahlay voo?
Can I come along?	Pouvez-vous m'emmener en voiture?
	poovay voo momuhnay ohn vwahtewr?
Can my boyfriend/ girlfriend come too?	Mon ami(e), peut-il/peut-elle venir avec nous?
	mawn nahmee, puh teel/puh tehl vuhneer ahvehk noo?
I'm trying to get to...	Je dois aller à...
	jhuh dwah zahlay ah...
Is that on the way to...?	C'est sur la route de...?
	seh sewr lah root duh...?
Could you drop me off...?	Vous pouvez me déposer...?
	voo poovay muh daypoazay...?
– here?	Vous pouvez me déposer ici?
	voo poovay muh daypoazay eesee?
– at the...exit?	Vous pouvez me déposer à la sortie vers...?
	voo poovay muh daypoazay ah lah sohrtee vehr...?
– in the centre?	Vous pouvez me déposer dans le centre?
	voo poovay muh daypoazay dohn luh sohntr?
– at the next roundabout?	Vous pouvez me déposer au prochain rond-point?
	voo poovay muh daypoazay oa proshahn rawnpwahn?

Could you stop here, please?	**Voulez-vous arrêter ici s'il vous plaît?**
	voolay voo zahrehtay eesee seel voo pleh?
I'd like to get out here	**Je voudrais descendre ici**
	jhuh voodreh duhsohndr eesee
Thanks for the lift	**Merci pour la route**
	mehrsee poor lah root

6.1 In general

● **You can check** departure times by telephone or minitel – a computerised information system widely available in France (for example in many post offices). Tickets for buses and the *métro* (Paris, Lyon and Marseille) are cheaper when bought in a *carnet* (book of ten), available at kiosks near some bus stops, at newsagents and in *métro* stations.

Announcements

Le train de...heures, en direction de... a un retard de... minutes.	The...train to...has been delayed by...minutes
Le train en direction de.../en provenance de...arrive sur le quai...	The train now arriving at platform...is the...train to .../from...
Le train en direction de...va quitter le quai...dans quelques instants.	The train to...is about to leave from platform...
Attention éloignez-vous de la voie, un train rapide va passer sur la voie...	Attention please, keep your distance from the rail track, an intercity train will pass on platform...
Nous approchons la gare de...	We're now approaching...

Where does this train go to?	Où va ce train? *oo vah suh trahn?*
Does this boat go to...?	Ce bateau, va-t-il à...? *suh bahtoa, vah teel ah...?*
Can I take this bus to...?	Puis-je prendre ce bus pour aller à...? *pwee jhuh prondr suh bews poor ahlay ah...?*

Does this train stop at...?	Ce train s'arrête-t-il à...?
	suh trahn sahreht-uh-teel ah...?
Is this seat taken/free/ reserved?	Est-ce que cette place est occupée/libre/réservée?
	ehs kuh seht plahs eh tokewpay/leebr/rayzehrvay?
I've booked...	J'ai réservé...
	jhay rayzehrvay...
Could you tell me where I have to get off for... ?	Voulez-vous me dire où descendre pour...?
	voolay voo muh deer oo duhsohndr poor...?
Could you let me know when we get to...?	Voulez-me prévenir lorsque nous serons à...?
	voolay voo muh prayvuhneer lorskuh noo suhrawn zah...?
Could you stop at the next stop, please?	Voulez-vous vous arrêter au prochain arrêt s'il vous plaît?
	voolay voo voo zahrehtay oa proshahn nahreht seel voo pleh?
Where are we now?	Où sommes-nous ici?
	oo som noo zeesee?
Do I have to get off here?	Dois-je descendre ici?
	dwah jhuh duhsohndr eesee?
Have we already passed...?	Avons-nous déjà dépassé...?
	ahvawn noo dayjhah daypahsay...?
How long have I been asleep?	Combien de temps ai-je dormi?
	kawnbyahn duh tohn ay jhuh dormee?
How long does... stop here?	Combien de temps...reste ici?
	kawnbyahn duh tohn...rehst eesee?
Can I come back on the same ticket?	Puis-je revenir avec ce billet?
	pwee jhuh ruhvuhneer ahvehk suh beeyeh?
Can I change on this ticket?	Puis-je prendre une correspondance avec ce billet?
	pwee jhuh prondr ewn korehspawndohns ahvehk suh beeyeh?

How long is this ticket__ valid for?	Combien de temps ce billet reste-t-il valable?
	kawnbyahn duh tohn suh beeyeh rehst-uh-teel vahlahbl?
How much is the _____ supplement for the TGV (high speed train)?	Combien coûte le supplément pour le TGV?
	kawnbyahn koot luh sewplaymohn poor luh tayjhayvay?

6.2 Questions to passengers

Ticket types

Première classe ou deuxième classe?	First or second class?
Aller simple ou retour?	Single or return?
Fumeurs ou non fumeurs?	Smoking or non-smoking?
Côté fenêtre ou côté couloir?	Window or aisle?
A l'avant ou à l'arrière?	Front or back?
Place assise ou couchette?	Seat or couchette?
Au-dessus, au milieu ou au-dessous?	Top, middle or bottom?
Classe touriste ou classe affaires?	Tourist class or business class?
Une cabine ou un fauteuil?	Cabin or seat?
Une personne ou deux personnes?	Single or double?
Vous êtes combien de personnes à voyager?	How many are travelling?

Destination

Où allez-vous?	Where are you travelling?
Quand partez-vous?	When are you leaving?
Votre...part à...	Your...leaves at...
Vous devez prendre une correspondance	You have to change trains
Vous devez descendre à...	You have to get off at...
Vous devez passer par...	You have to travel via...
L'aller est le..	The outward journey is on...
Le retour est le...	The return journey is on...
Vous devez être à bord au plus tard à...	You have to be on board by...

On board

Votre billet s'il vous plaît	Your ticket, please
Votre réservation s'il vous plaît	Your reservation, please
Votre passeport s'il vous plaît	Your passport, please
Vous n'êtes pas à la bonne place	You're in the wrong seat
Vous êtes dans le mauvais...	You're on/in the wrong...
Cette place est réservée	This seat is reserved
Vous devez payer un supplément	You'll have to pay a supplement
Le...a un retard de...minutes	The...has been delayed by...minutes

6.3 Tickets

Where can I...? _____	Où puis-je...?
	oo pwee jhuh...?
– buy a ticket? _____	Où puis-je acheter un billet?
	oo pwee jhahshtay uhn beeyeh?
– make a reservation?__	Où puis-je réserver une place?
	oo pwee jhuh rayzehrvay ewn plahs?
– book a flight?_____	Où puis-je réserver un vol?
	oo pwee jhuh rayzehrvay uhn vol?
Could I have a...to..., ___ please?	Puis-je avoir...en direction de...?
	pwee jhahvwahr...ohn deerehksyawn duh...?
– a single _____	Puis-je avoir un aller simple?
	pwee jhahvwahr uhn nahlay sahnpl?
– a return _____	Puis-je avoir un aller-retour?
	pwee jhahvwahr uhn nahlay ruhtoor?
first class _____	première classe
	pruhmyehr klahs
second class_____	deuxième classe
	duhzyehm klahs
tourist class_____	classe touriste
	klahs tooreest
business class _____	classe affaires
	klahs ahfehr
I'd like to book a _____ seat/couchette/cabin	Je voudrais réserver une place assise/couchette/cabine
	jhuh voodreh rayzehrvay ewn plahs ahseez/koosheht/kahbeen
I'd like to book a berth _ in the sleeping car	Je voudrais réserver une place dans le wagon-lit
	jhuh voodreh rayzehrvay ewn plahs dohn luh vahgawnlee
top/middle/bottom_____	au-dessus/au milieu/au-dessous
	oaduhsew/ oa meelyuh/ oa duhsoo

smoking/no smoking ___	fumeurs/non fumeurs
	fewmuhr/ nawn fewmuhr
by the window _____	à côté de la fenêtre
	ah koatay duh lah fenehtr
single/double _____	une personne/deux personnes
	ewn pehrson/duh pehrson
at the front/back_____	à l'avant/à l'arrière
	ah lahvohn/ah lahryehr
There are...of us _____	Nous sommes...personnes
	noo som...pehrson
a car _____	une voiture
	ewn vwahtewr
a caravan_____	une caravane
	ewn kahrahvahnn
...bicycles_____	...bicyclettes
	...beeseekleht
Do you also have...? ___	Avez-vous aussi...?
	ahvay voo zoasee...?
– season tickets? _____	Avez-vous aussi une carte d'abonnement?
	ahvay voo zoasee ewn kahrt dahbonmohn?
– weekly tickets? _____	Avez-vous aussi une carte hebdomadaire?
	ahvay voo zoasee ewn kahrt ehbdomahdehr?
– monthly season_____ tickets?	Avez-vous aussi une carte mensuelle?
	ahvay voo zoasee ewn kahrt mohnsewehl?

6.4 Information

Where's? _____	Où se trouve...?
	oo suh troov...?

Where's the _____ information desk?	Où se trouve le bureau de renseignements?
	oo suh troov luh bewroa duh rohnsehnyuhmohn?
Where can I find a _____ timetable?	Où se trouvent les horaires des départs/des arrivées?
	oo se troov lay zorehr day daypahr/day zahreevay?
Where's the...desk? _____	Où se trouve la réception de...?
	oo se troov lah raysehpsyawn duh...?
Do you have a city _____ map with the bus/the underground routes on it?	Avez-vous un plan du réseau des bus/du métro?
	ahvay voo zuhn plohn dew rayzoa day bews/dew maytroa?
Do you have a _____ timetable?	Avez-vous un horaire des arrivées et des départs?
	ahvay voo zuhn norehr day zahreevay ay day daypahr?
I'd like to confirm/ _____ cancel/change my booking for...	Je veux confirmer/annuler/changer ma réservation pour...
	jhuh vuh kawnfeermay/ahnewlay/shohnjhay mah rayzehrvahsyawn poor...
Will I get my money _____ back?	Mon argent me sera rendu?
	mawn nahrjhohn muh suhrah rohndew?
I want to go to..._____ How do I get there? (What's the quickest way there?)	Je dois aller à...Comment puis-je y aller (le plus vite possible)?
	jhuh dwah zahlay ah...komohn pwee jhee ahlay (luh plew veet poseebl?)
How much is a _____ single/return to...?	Combien coûte un aller simple/un aller-retour pour...?
	kawnbyahn koot uhn nahlay sahnpl/uhn nahlay retoor poor...?
Do I have to pay a _____ supplement?	Dois-je payer un supplément?
	dwah jheuh payay uhn sewplaymohn?

Can I interrupt my ___ journey with this ticket?	Puis-je interrompre mon voyage avec ce billet?
	pwee jhahntayrawnpr mawn vwahyahjh ahvehk suh beeyeh?
How much luggage ___ am I allowed?	J'ai droit à combien de bagages?
	jhay drwah ah kawnbyahn duh bahgahjh?
Does this...travel ___ direct?	Ce...est direct?
	suh...eh deerehkt?
Do I have to change? __ Where?	Dois-je changer? Où?
	dwah jhuh shohnjhay? oo?
Will this plane make ___ any stopovers?	L'avion fait escale?
	lahvyawn feh tehskahl?
Does the boat call in at_ any ports on the way?	Est-ce que le bateau fait escale dans un port pendant son trajet?
	ehs kuh luh bahtoa feh tehskahl dohn zuhn por pohndohn sawn trahjheh?
Does the train/ ___ bus stop at...?	Est-ce que le train/le bus s'arrête à...?
	ehs kuh luh trahn/luh bews sahreht ah...?
Where should I get off?_	Où dois-je descendre?
	oo dwah jhuh duhsohndr?
Is there a connection___ to...?	Y a-t-il une correspondance pour...?
	ee yah teel ewn korehspawndohns poor...?
How long do I have to__ wait?	Combien de temps dois-je attendre?
	kawnbyahn duh tohn dwah jhahtohndr?
When does...leave? ___	Quand part...? *kohn pahr...?*
What time does the ___ first/next/last...leave?	A quelle heure part le premier/prochain/dernier...?
	ah kehl uhr pahr luh pruhmyay/proshahn/dehrnyay...?
How long does...take? _	Combien de temps met le...?
	kawnbyahn duh tohn meh luh...?
What time does...arrive_ in...?	A quelle heure arrive...à...?
	ah kehl uhr ahreev...ah...?
Where does the...to... __ leave from?	D'où part le...pour...?
	doo pahr luh...poor...?
Is this...to...? ___	Est-ce le...pour...?
	ehs luh...poor...?

6.5 Aeroplanes

● **At arrival** at a French airport (*aéroport*), you will find the following signs:

arrivée	départ
arrivals	departures

6.6 Trains

● **The rail network** is extensive. *La Société Nationale des Chemins de Fer Français (SNCF)* is responsible for the national rail traffic. Besides the normal train, there is also *le Train à Grande Vitesse (TGV)* for which you will have to pay a supplement. Reservations before departure are cheaper. The TGV operates between the larger cities: Paris, Lyon, Marseille and Nice. A train ticket has to be stamped (*composté*) before departure.

6.7 Taxis

● **In nearly all** large cities, there are plenty of taxis. French taxis have no fixed colour. Virtually all taxis have a meter. In the smaller towns, it is usual to agree a fixed price in advance. A supplement is usual for luggage, a journey at night, on a Sunday or Bank holiday, or to an airport. It is advisable in large cities such as Paris and Lyon to check that the meter has been returned to zero at the start of the journey.

libre	occupé	station de taxis
for hire	booked	taxi rank

Taxi! _____	**Taxi!** *tahksee!*
Could you get me a ___ taxi, please?	**Pouvez-vous m'appeler un taxi?** *poovay voo mahpuhlay uhn tahksee?*
Where can I find a taxi _ around here?	**Où puis-je prendre un taxi par ici?** *oo pwee jhuh prohndr uhn tahksee pahr eesee?*
Could you take me _____ to..., please?	**Conduisez-moi à...s'il vous plaît.** *kawndweezay mwah ah...seel voo pleh*
– this address _____	**Conduisez-moi à cette adresse.** *kawndweezay mwah ah seht ahdrehs*
– the...hotel _____	**Conduisez-moi à l'hôtel...** *kawndweezay mwah ah loatehl...*
– the town/city centre __	**Conduisez-moi dans le centre.** *kawndweezay mwah dohn luh sohntr*
– the station _____	**Conduisez-moi à la gare.** *kawndweezay mwah ah lah gahr*
– the airport_____	**Conduisez-moi à l'aéroport.** *kawndweezay mwah ah layroapor.*
How much is the _____ trip to...?	**Combien coûte un trajet jusqu'à...?** *kawnbyahn koot uhn trahjheh jhewskah...?*
How far is it to...?_____	**C'est combien de kilomètres jusqu'à...?** *seh kawnbyahn duh keeloamehtr jhewskah...?*
Could you turn on the __ meter, please?	**Voulez-vous mettre le compteur en marche s'il vous plaît?** *voolay voo mehtr luh kawntuhr ohn mahrsh seel voo pleh?*
I'm in a hurry_____	**Je suis pressé.** *jhuh swee prehssay*
Could you speed _____ up/slow down a little?	**Vous pouvez rouler plus vite/plus lentement?** *voo poovay roolay plew veet/plew lohntmohn?*
Could you take a _____ different route?	**Vous pouvez prendre une autre route?** *voo poovay prohndr ewn oatr root?*

I'd like to get out here, please	**Je voudrais descendre ici**
	jhuh voodreh duhsohndr eesee
You have to go...here	**Là vous allez...**
	lah voo zahlay...
You have to go straight on here	**Là vous allez tout droit**
	lah voo zahlay too drwah
You have to turn left here	**Là vous allez à gauche**
	lah voo zahlay zah goash
You have to turn right here	**Là vous allez à droite**
	lah voo zahlay zah drwaht
This is it	**C'est ici**
	seht eesee
Could you wait a minute for me, please?	**Vous pouvez m'attendre un instant?**
	voo poovay mahtohndr uhn nahnstohn?

Overnight accommodation

7.1 General

● **There is great variety** of overnight accommodation in France.
Hôtels: stars indicate the degree of comfort; from five stars, the most luxurious, to one star, very simple. Beside the star one often finds the letters NN-Nouvelles Normes (new classifications). This means that the star-classification is up-to-date. Most hotels offer *pension complète* (full board) or *demi-pension* (half board).
Auberges et Relais de campagne: luxurious; splendid view and lots of rest are guaranteed.
Châteaux, Hôtels de France and Vieilles Demeures: a very expensive tourist residence, always within a castle, country manor or an historic building.
Logis de France: an organisation with many hotels with one or two stars, mostly outside the town centre. The hotel can be recognised by the yellow signboards with a green fireplace and the words: logis de France.
Motels: especially along the motorway, comparable to UK motels.
Auberges de jeunesse (youth hostel): the number of nights is restricted to between three and seven.
Camping: free camping is allowed, except for forest areas with the sign *attention au feu* (fire hazard). Not all camping sites are guarded.
Refuges et gîtes d'étape (mountain huts): in the Alps and Pyrenees. These huts are owned by the *Club Alpin Français* and are inexpensive.

Combien de temps voulez-vous rester?	How long do you want to stay?
Voulez-vous remplir ce questionnaire s'il vous plaît?	Fill out this form, please
Puis-je avoir votre passeport?	Could I see your passport?
Vous devez payer un acompte	I'll need a deposit
Vous devez payer à l'avance	You'll have to pay in advance

My name's...I've made _____ a reservation over the phone/by mail	**Mon nom est...J'ai réservé une place par téléphone/par lettre** *mawn nawn eh...jhay rayzehrvay ewn plahs pahr taylayfon/pahr lehtr*
How much is it per _____ night/week/ month?	**Quel est le prix pour une nuit/une semaine/un mois?** *kehl eh luh pree poor ewn nwee/ewn suhmehn/uhn mwah?*
We'll be staying at _____ least...nights/weeks	**Nous restons au moins...nuits/semaines.** *noo rehstawn zoa mwhan...nwee/suhmehn*
We don't know yet_____	**Nous ne le savons pas encore exactement.** *noo nuh luh sahvawn pah zohnkor ehgzahktmohn*
Do you allow pets _____ (cats/dogs)?	**Est-ce que les animaux domestiques(chiens/chats) sont admis?** *ehs kuh lay zahneemoa domehsteek(shyahn/shah) sawn tahdmee?*
What time does the _____ gate/door open/close?	**A quelle heure on ouvre/ferme le portail/la porte?** *ah keh uhr awn noovr/fehrm luh portahy/lah port?*
Could you get me _____ a taxi, please?	**Vous voulez m'appeler un taxi?** *voo voolay mahplay uhn tahksee?*
Is there any mail_____ for me?	**Y a-t-il du courrier pour moi?** *ee yah teel dew kooryay poor mwah?*

7.2 Camping

Where's the manager? _	**Où est le gardien?** *oo eh luh gahrdyahn?*
Are we allowed to _____ camp here?	**Pouvons-nous camper ici?** *poovawn noo kohnpay eesee?*

Vous pouvez vous-même choisir votre emplacement.	You can pick your own site
Votre emplacement vous sera attribué.	You'll be allocated a site
Voici votre numéro d'emplacement.	This is your site number
Vous devez coller ceci sur votre voiture.	Stick this on your car, please
Ne perdez surtout pas cette carte.	Please don't lose this card

There are...of us and ...tents	Nous sommes...personnes et nous avons...tentes.
	noo som...pehrson ay nooz ahvawn...tohnt
Can we pick our own place?	Pouvons-nous choisir nous-mêmes un emplacement?
	poovawn noo shwahzeer noo mehm uhn nohnplahsmohn?
Do you have a quiet spot for us?	Avez-vous un endroit calme pour nous?
	ahvay voo zuhn nohndrwah kahlm poor noo?
Do you have any other pitches available?	Vous n'avez pas d'autre emplacement libre?
	voo nahvay pah doatr ohnplahsmohn leebr?
It's too windy/sunny/ shady here.	Ici il y a trop de vent/soleil/ombre.
	eesee eel ee yah troa duh vohn/sohlehy/awnbr
It's too crowded here	Il y a trop de monde ici.
	eel ee yah troa duh mawnd eesee
The ground's too hard/uneven	Le sol est trop dur/irrégulier.
	luh sohl eh troa dewr/eeraygewlyay

Do you have a level spot for the camper/caravan/folding caravan?	Avez-vous un endroit plat pour le camping-car/la caravane/la caravane pliante?
	ahvay voo zuhn nohndrwah plah poor luh kohnpeeng kahr/lah kahrahvahnn/lah kahrahvahnn plyohnt?
Could we have adjoining pitches?	Pouvons-nous être l'un à côté de l'autre?
	poovawn noo zehtr luhn nah koatay duh loatr?
Can we park the car next to the tent?	La voiture, peut-elle être garée à côté de la tente?
	lah vwahtewr, puh tehl ehtr gahray ah koatay duh lah tohnt?
How much is it per person/tent/caravan/car?	Quel est le prix par personne/tente/caravane/voiture?
	kehl eh luh pree pahr pehrson/tohnt/kahrahvahnn/vwahtewr?
Are there any...?	Y a-t-il...?
	ee yah teel...?
– any hot showers?	Y a-t-il des douches avec eau chaude?
	ee yah teel day doosh ahvehk oa shoad?
– washing machines?	Y a-t-il des machines à laver?
	ee yah teel day mahsheen ah lahvay?
Is there a...on the site?	Y a-t-il un...sur le terrain?
	ee ayh teel uhn...sewr luh tehrahn?
Is there a children's play area on the site?	Y a-t-il un terrain de jeux pour les enfants?
	ee yah teel uhn tehrahn duh jhuh poor lay zohnfohn?
Are there covered cooking facilities on the site?	Y a-t-il un endroit couvert pour cuisiner?
	ee yah teel uhn nohndrwa koovehr poor kweezeenay?
Can I rent a safe here?	Puis-je louer un coffre-fort ici?
	pwee jhuh looay uhn kofr for eesee?
Are we allowed to barbecue here?	Pouvons-nous faire un barbecue?
	poovawn noo fehr uhn bahrbuhkew?

Are there any power ____   Y a-t-il des prises électriques?
points?   *ee yah teel day preez aylehktreek?*

Is there drinking _____   Y a-t-il de l'eau potable?
water?   *ee yah teel duh loa potabl?*

When's the rubbish ____   Quand vide-t-on les poubelles?
collected?   *kohn veed-uh-tawn lay poobehl?*

Do you sell gas bottles _   Vendez-vous des bouteilles de gaz
(butane gas/propane   (butane/propane)?
gas)?   *vohnday voo day bootehuhy duh gahz*
  (bewtahnn/propahnn)?

7.3 Hotel/B&B/apartment/holiday house

Do you have a _____   Avez-vous une chambre libre pour une
single/double room   personne/deux personnes?
available?   *ahvay voo zewn shohnbr leebr poor ewn*
  pehrson/duh pehrson?

per person/per room ___   par personne/par chambre
  pahr pehrson/pahr shohnbr

Does that include_____   Est-ce que le petit déjeuner/le déjeuner/le
breakfast/lunch/   dîner est compris?
dinner?   *ehs kuh luh puhtee dayjhuhnay/luh*
  dayjhuhnay/luh deenay eh kawnpree?

Could we have two ____   Pouvons-nous avoir deux chambres
adjoining rooms?   contiguës?
  poovawn noo zahvwahr duh shohnbr
  kawnteegew?

with/without_____   avec/sans toilettes/salle de bains/douche
toilet/bath/shower   *ahvehk/sohn twahleht/sahl duh bahn/doosh*

(not) facing the street _   (pas) du côté rue
  (pah) dew koatay rew

with/without a view ____   avec/sans vue sur la mer
of the sea   *ahvehk/sohn vew sewr lah mehr*

Camping equipment

luggage space	l'espace (f.) bagages	*lehspahs bahgajh*
can opener	l'ouvre-boîte (m.)	*loovr bwaht*
butane gas bottle	la bouteille de butane	*lah bootehy duh bewtahnn*
pannier	la sacoche de vélo	*lah sahkosh duh vayloa*
gas cooker	le réchaud à gaz	*luh rayshoa ah gahz*
groundsheet	le tapis de sol	*luh tahpee duh sol*
mallet	le marteau	*luh mahrtoa*
hammock	le hamac	*luh ahmahk*
jerry can	le bidon d'essence	*luh beedawn dehssohns*
campfire	le feu de camp	*luh fuh duh kohn*
folding chair	la chaise pliante	*lah shehz plyohnt*
insulated picnic box	la glacière	*lah glahsyehr*
ice pack	le bac à glaçons	*luh bah kah glasawn*
compass	la boussole	*lah boosol*
wick	la mèche	*lah mehsh*
corkscrew	le tire-bouchon	*luh teer booshawn*
airbed	le matelas pneumatique	*luh mahtuhlah pnuhmahteek*
airbed plug	le bouchon du matelas pneumatique	*luh booshawn dew mahtuhlah pnemahteek*
pump	la pompe à air	*lah pawnp ah ehr*

Is there...in the hotel? __ Y a-t-il...dans l'hôtel?
ee yah teel...dohn loatehl?

Is there a lift in the _____ Y a-t-il un ascenseur dans l'hôtel?
hotel? *ee yah teel uhn nahsohnsuhr dohn loatehl?*

awning	l'auvent (m.)	*loavohn*
karimat	la natte	*lah naht*
pan	la casserole	*lah kahsrol*
pan handle	la poignée de casserole	*lah pwahnnyay duh kahsrol*
primus stove	le réchaud à pétrole	*luh rayshoa ah paytrol*
zip	la fermeture éclair	*lah fehrmuhtewr ayklehr*
backpack	le sac à dos	*luh sahk ah doa*
guy rope	la corde	*lah kord*
sleeping bag	le sac de couchage	*luh sahk duh kooshajh*
storm lantern	a lanterne-tempête	*lah lohntehrn-tohnpeht*
camp bed	e lit de camp	*luh lee duh kohn*
table	la table	*lah tahbl*
tent	la tente	*lah tohnt*
tent peg	le piquet	*luh peekeh*
tent pole	le mât	*luh mah*
vacuum flask	la bouteille thermos	*lah bootehy tehrmos*
water bottle	la gourde	*lah goord*
clothes peg	la pince à linge	*lah pahns ah lahnjh*
windbreak	le pare-vent	*luh pahrvohn*
torch	la torche électrique	*lah torsh aylehktreek*
pocket knife	le canif	*luh kahneef*

Do you have room _____ service?

Y a-t-il un service de chambre dans l'hôtel?
ee yah teel uhn sehrvees duh shohnbr dohn loatehl?

Les toilettes et la douche sont au même étage/dans votre chambre
You can find the toilet and shower on the same floor/en suite

De ce côté, s'il vous plaît
This way, please

Votre chambre est au...étage, c'est le numéro...
Your room is on the...floor, number...

Could I see the room?	**Puis-je voir la chambre?** *pwee jhuh vwhar lah shohnbr?*
I'll take this room	**Je prends cette chambre.** *jhuh prohn seht shohnbr*
We don't like this one	**Celle-ci ne nous plaît pas.** *sehl see nuh noo pleh pah*
Do you have a larger/ less expensive room?	**Avez-vous une chambre plus grande/moins chère?** *avay voo zewn shohnbr plew grohnd/mwahn shehr?*
Could you put in a cot?	**Pouvez-vous y ajouter un lit d'enfant?** *poovay voo zee ahjhootay uhn lee dohnfohn?*
What time's breakfast?	**A quelle heure est le petit déjeuner?** *ah kehl uhr eh luh puhtee dayjhuhnay?*
Where's the dining room?	**Où est la salle à manger?** *oo eh lah sahl ah mohnjhay?*
Can I have breakfast in my room?	**Puis-je prendre le petit déjeuner dans la chambre?** *pwee jhuh prohndr luh puhtee dayjhuhnay dohn lah shohnbr?*
Where's the emergency exit/fire escape?	**Où est la sortie de secours/l'escalier de secours?** *oo eh lah sortee duh suhkoor/lehskahlyay duh suhkoor?*

Where can I park my ___ car (safely)?	Où puis-je garer ma voiture (en sécurité)? *oo pwee jhuh gahray mah vwahtewr (ohn saykewreetay)?*
The key to room..., ___ please	La clef de la chambre..., s'il vous plaît. *lah klay duh lah shohnbr...,seel voo pleh*
Could you put this in ___ the safe, please?	Puis-je mettre ceci dans votre coffre-fort? *pwee jhuh mehtr suhsee dohn votr kofr for?*
Could you wake me___ at...tomorrow?	Demain voulez-vous me réveiller à...heures? *duhmahn voolay voo muh rayvehyay ah...uhr?*
Could you find a___ babysitter for me?	Pouvez-vous m'aider à trouver une baby-sitter? *poovay voo mayday ah troovay ewn behbee seetehr?*
Could I have an extra ___ blanket?	Puis-je avoir une couverture supplémentaire? *pwee jhahvwahr ewn koovehrtewr sewplaymohntehr?*
What days do the___ cleaners come in?	Quels jours fait-on le ménage? *kehl jhoor feh tawn luh maynahjh?*
When are the sheets/ ___ towels/tea towels changed?	Quand change-t-on les draps/les serviettes-éponge/les torchons? *kohn shohnjh tawn lay drah/lay sehrvyeht aypawnjh/lay tohrshawn?*

7.4 Complaints

We can't sleep for ___ the noise	Nous ne pouvons pas dormir à cause du bruit *noo nuh poovawn pah dormeer ah koaz dew brwee*

103

Could you turn the_____ radio down, please?	Est-ce que vous pouvez baisser un peu la radio? *ehs kuh voo poovay behssay uhn puh lah rahdyoa?*
We're out of toilet_____ paper	Il n'y a plus de papier hygiénique *eel nee yah plew duh pahpyay eejhyayneek*
There aren't_____ any.../there's not enough...	Il n'y a pas de/pas assez de... *eel nee yah pah duh/pah zahsay duh...*
The bed linen's dirty ___	La literie est sale *lah leetree eh sahl*
The room hasn't been __ cleaned	La chambre n'a pas été nettoyée *lah shohnbr nah pah zaytay nehtwahyay*
The kitchen is not _____ clean	La cuisine n'est pas propre *lah kweezeen neh pah propr*
The kitchen utensils____ are dirty	Les ustensiles de cuisine sont sales *lay zewstohnseel duh kweezeen sawn sahl*
The heater's not _____ working	Le chauffage ne marche pas *luh shoafajh nuh marsh pah*
There's no (hot)_____ water/electricity	Il n'y a pas d'eau(chaude)/d'électricité *eel nee yah pah doa(shoad)/daylehktreeseetay*
...is broken_____	...est cassé *...eh kahssay*
Could you have that ___ seen to?	Vous pouvez le faire réparer? *voo poovay luh fehr raypahray?*
Could I have another___ room/site?	Puis-je avoir une autre chambre/un autre emplacement pour la tente? *pwee jhuh ahvwahr ewn oatr shohnbr/uhn noatr ohnplasmohn poor lah tohnt?*
The bed creaks terribly _	Le lit grince énormément *luh lee grahns aynormaymohn*
The bed sags _____	Le lit s'affaisse *luh lee sahfehs*

There are bugs/insects in our room	Nous sommes incommodés par des bestioles/insectes
	noo som zahnkomoday pahr day behstyol/day zahnsehkt
This place is full of mosquitos	C'est plein de moustiques ici
	seh plahn duh moosteek eesee
– cockroaches	C'est plein de cafards
	seh plahn duh kahfahr

7.5 Departure

See also 8.2 Settling the bill

I'm leaving tomorrow. Could I settle my bill, please?	Je pars demain. Puis-je payer maintenant?
	jhuh pahr duhmahn. pwee jhuh payay mahntuhnohn?
What time should we vacate?	A quelle heure devons-nous quitter la chambre?
	ah kehl uhr duhvawn noo keetay lah shohnbr?
Could I have my passport back, please?	Pouvez-vous me rendre mon passeport?
	poovay voo muh rohndr mawn pahspor?
We're in a terrible hurry	Nous sommes très pressés
	noo som treh prehssay
Could you forward my mail to this address?	Pouvez-vous faire suivre mon courrier à cette adresse?
	poovay voo fehr sweevr mawn kooryay ah seht ahdrehs?
Could we leave our luggage here until we leave?	Nos valises peuvent rester ici jusqu'à notre départ?
	noa vahleez puhv rehstay eesee jhewskah notr daypahr?
Thanks for your hospitality	Merci pour votre hospitalité
	mehrsee poor votr ospeetahleetay

8 Money matters

● **In general**, banks are open 9–12 and 2–4pm; they are closed on Saturdays. In city centres they are often open at lunchtime. In tourist areas, the bank can be closed on Monday morning and open on Saturday morning. To exchange currency a proof of identity is usually required. The sign *Change* indicates that money can be exchanged.

8.1 Banks

Where can I find a _____ bank/an exchange office around here?	Où puis-je trouver une banque/un bureau de change par ici?
	oo pwee jhuh troovay ewn bohnk/uhn bewroa duh shohnjh pahr eesee?
Where can I cash this __ traveller's cheque/giro cheque?	Où puis-je encaisser ce chèque de voyage/chèque postal?
	oo pwee jhuh ohnkehssay suh shehk duh vwahyajh/shehk postahl?
Can I cash this...here? _	Puis-je encaisser ce...ici?
	pweejh ohnkehssay suh...eesee?
Can I withdraw money _ on my credit card here?	Puis-je retirer de l'argent avec une carte de crédit?
	pwee jhuh ruhteeray duh lahrjhohn ahvehk ewn kahrt duh kraydee?
What's the minimum/ __ maximum amount?	Quel est le montant minimum/maximum?
	kehl eh luh mohntohn meeneemuhm/mahxseemuhm?
Can I take out less_____ than that?	Puis-je retirer moins?
	pwee jhuh ruhteeray mwahn?
I've had some money __ transferred here. Has it arrived yet?	J'ai fait virer de l'argent par mandat télégraphique. Est-ce déjà arrivé?
	jhay feh veeray duh lahrjhohn pahr mohndah taylaygrahfeek. ehs dayjhah ahreevay?
These are the details ___ of my bank in the UK	Voici les coordonnées de ma banque au Royaume-Uni
	vwahsee lay koa-ordonay duh mah bohnk oa rwahyoam ewnee

Vous devez signer ici	You have to sign here
Vous devez remplir ceci	You have to fill this out
Puis-je voir votre passeport?	Could I see your passport?
Puis-je voir une pièce d'identité?	Could I see some identification?
Puis-je voir votre carte de chèque postal?	Could I see your girobank card?
Puis-je voir votre carte bancaire?	Could I see your bank card?

This is my bank/giro account number — **Voici mon numéro de compte bancaire/numéro de chèque postal** *vwahsee mawn newmayroa duh kawnt bohnkehr/newmayroa duh shehk postahl*

I'd like to change some money — **J'aimerais changer de l'argent** *jhehmuhreh shohnjhay duh lahrjhohn*

– pounds into... — **des livres sterling contre...** *day leevr stehrleeng kawntr...*

– dollars into... — **des dollars contre...** *day dolahr kawntr...*

What's the exchange rate? — **Le change est à combien?** *luh shohnjh eh tah kawnbyahn?*

Could you give me some small change with it? — **Pouvez-vous me donner de la monnaie?** *poovay voo muh donay duh lah moneh?*

This is not right — **Ce n'est pas exact** *suh neh pah zehgzah.*

8.2 Settling the bill

Could you put it on my bill? — **Pouvez-vous le mettre sur mon compte?** *poovay voo luh mehtr sewr mawn kawnt?*

Does this amount include service? — **Est-ce que le service est compris(dans la somme)?** *ehs kuh luh sehrvees eh kawnpree(dohn lah som)?*

Can I pay by...? _____	**Puis-je payer avec…?**
	pwee jhuh payay ahvehk...?
Can I pay by credit card? _____	**Puis-je payer avec une carte de crédit?**
	pwee jhuh payay ahvehk ewn kahrt duh kraydee?
Can I pay by traveller's _ cheque?	**Puis-je payer avec un chèque de voyage?**
	pwee jhuh payay ahvehk uhn shehk duh vwahyajh?
Can I pay with foreign __ currency?	**Puis-je vous payer en devises étrangères?**
	pwee jhuh voo payay ohn duhveez aytrohnjhehr?
You've given me too ____ much/you haven't given me enough change	**Vous m'avez trop/pas assez rendu**
	voo mahvay troa/pah zahsay rohndew
Could you check this ___ again, please?	**Voulez-vous refaire le calcul?**
	voolay voo ruhfehr luh kahlkewl?
Could I have a receipt, _ please?	**Pouvez-vous me donner un reçu/le ticket de caisse?**
	poovay voo muh donay uhn ruhsew/luh teekeh duh kehs?
I don't have enough_____ money on me	**Je n'ai pas assez d'argent sur moi**
	jhuh nay pah zahsay dahrjhohn sewr mwah
This is for you _____	**Voilà, c'est pour vous**
	vwahlah seh poor voo
Keep the change _____	**Gardez la monnaie**
	gahrday lah moneh

Nous n'acceptons pas les cartes de crédit/les chèques de voyage/les devises étrangères	Credit cards/traveller's cheques/foreign currency are not accepted

9

Post and telephone

9.1 Post

For giros, see 8 Money matters

● **Post offices** are open from Monday to Friday between 8am and 7pm. In smaller towns the post office closes at lunch. On Saturday they are open between 8am and 12 noon.
Stamps *(timbres)* are also available in a *tabac* (café that sells cigarettes and matches).
The yellow letter box *(boîte aux lettres)* in the street and in the post office has two rates: *tarif normal* (normal rate) and *tarif réduit* (reduced rate).
It is advisable to opt for the *tarif normal.*

colis	télégrammes	timbres
parcels	telegrams	stamps
mandats		
money orders		

Where's...?_____	Où est...?
	oo eh...?
Where's the post office?	Où est la poste?
	oo eh lah post?
Where's the main post _ office?	Où est la poste centrale?
	oo eh lah post sohntrahl?
Where's the postbox? __	Où est la boîte aux lettres?
	oo eh lah bwaht oa lehtr?
Which counter should __ I go to...?	Quel est le guichet pour...?
	kehl eh luh gueesheh poor...?
– to send a fax _____	Quel est le guichet pour les fax?
	kehl eh luh gueesheh poor lay fahx?

– to change money	**Quel est le guichet pour changer de l'argent?**
	kehl eh luh gueesheh poor shohnjhay duh lahrjhohn?
-to change giro cheques	**Quel est le guichet pour les chèques postaux?**
	kehl eh luh gueesheh poor lay shehk postoa?
-for a telegraph money order?	**Quel est le guichet pour faire un virement postal télégraphique?**
	kehl eh luh gueesheh poor fehr uhn veermohn postahl taylaygrahfeek?
Poste restante	**Poste restante**
	post rehstohnt
Is there any mail for me? My name's...	**Y a-t-il du courrier pour moi? Mon nom est…**
	ee yah teel dew kooryay poor mwah? mawn nawn eh…

Stamps

What's the postage for a...to...?	**Combien faut-il sur une…pour...?**
	kawnbyahn foa teel sewr ewn…poor…?
Are there enough stamps on it?	**Y a-t-il suffisamment de timbres dessus?**
	ee yah teel sewfeezahmohn duh tahnbr duhsew?
I'd like... ...euro stamps	**Je voudrais...timbres à...**
	jhuh voodreh…tahnbr ah…
I'd like to send this...	**Je veux envoyer ce/cette…**
	jhuh vuh zohnvwahyay suh/seht…
– express	**Je veux envoyer ce/cette...en express.**
	jhuh vuh zohnvwahyay suh/seht…ohn nehxprehs
– by air mail	**Je veux envoyer ce/cette...par avion.**
	jhuh vuh zohnvwahyay suh/seht…pahr ahvyawn

| – by registered mail ____ | **Je veux envoyer ce/cette...en recommandé.** |
| | *jhuh vuh zohnvwahyay suh/seht...ohn ruhkomohnday* |

Telegram / fax

I'd like to send a_____ telegram to...	**J'aimerais envoyer un télégramme à...**
	jhehmuhreh zohnvwahyay uhn taylaygrahm ah...
How much is that_____ per word?	**C'est combien par mot?**
	seh kawnbyahn pahr moa?
This is the text I want __ to send	**Voici le texte que je veux envoyer.**
	vwahsee luh tehxt kuh jhuh vuh zohnvwahyay
Shall I fill out the form __ myself?	**Puis-je remplir le questionnaire moi-même?**
	pwee jhuh rohnpleer luh kehstyonehr mwah mehm?
Can I make _____ photocopies/ send a fax here?	**Puis-je faire des photocopies/envoyer un fax ici?**
	pwee jhuh fehr day foatoakopee/ ohnvwahyay uhn fahx eesee?

9.2 Telephone

See also 1.8 Telephone alphabet

● **All phone booths** offer a direct international service to the UK or the US (00 + country code 44[UK] or 1[US]+ trunk code minus zero + number). Most phone booths will only accept phone cards *(télécartes)*, which can be bought at the post office or in a *tabac*. Phone booths do not take incoming calls. Charges can no longer be reversed in France. A *carte globéo* (special card) can be obtained from any office of the telephone company, on presentation of a credit card and identification. Charges are then deducted from the bank account. When phoning someone in France, you will not be greeted with the subscriber's name, but with *allô* or *allô oui?*

Is there a phone box ___ around here?	Y a-t-il une cabine téléphonique dans le coin?
	ee ah teel ewn kahbeen taylayfoneek dohn luh kwahn?
Could I use your_____ phone, please?	Puis-je utiliser votre téléphone?
	pwee jhuh ewteeleezay votr taylayfon?
Do you have a _____ (city/region)...phone directory?	Avez-vous un annuaire de la ville de.../de la région de...?
	ahvay voo zuhn ahnnewehr duh lah veel duh.../duh lah rayjhyawn duh...?
Where can I get a_____ phone card?	Où puis-je acheter une télécarte?
	oo pwee jhahshtay ewn taylaykahrt?
Could you give me...? __	Pouvez-vous me donner...?
	poovay voo muh donay...?
– the number for_____ international directory enquiries	Pouvez-vous me donner le numéro des renseignements pour l'étranger?
	poovay voo muh donay luh newmayroa day rohnsehnyuhmohn poor laytrohnjhay?
– the number of _____ room...	Pouvez-vous me donner le numéro de la chambre...?
	poovay voo muh donay luh newmayroa duh lah shohnbr...?
– the international _____ access code	Pouvez-vous me donner le numéro international?
	poovay voo muh donay luh newmayroa ahntehrnahsyonahl?
– the country code_____ for...	Pouvez-vous me donner l'indicatif du pays pour...?
	poovay voo muh donay lahndeekahteef dew payee poor...?
– the trunk code for... __	Pouvez-vous me donner l'indicatif de...?
	poovay voo muh donay lahndeekahteef duh...?
– the number of..._____	Pouvez-vous me donner le numéro d'abonné de...?
	poovay voo muh donay luh newmayroa dahbonay duh...?

Could you check if this this number's correct?	Pouvez-vous vérifier si ce numéro est correct? *poovay voo vayreefay see suh newmayroa eh korehkt?*
Can I dial international direct?	Puis-je téléphoner en automatique à l'étranger? *pwee jhuh taylayfonay ohn noatoamahteek ah laytrohnjhay?*
Do I have to go through the switchboard?	Dois-je appeler en passant par le standard? *dwah jhahpuhlay ohn pahsohn pahr luh stohndahr?*
Do I have to dial '0' first?	Dois-je d'abord faire le zéro? *dwah jhuh dahbor fehr luh zayroa?*
Do I have to book my calls?	Dois-je demander ma communication? *dwah jhuh duhmohnday mah komewneekahsyawn?*
Could you dial this number for me, please?	Voulez-vous m'appeler ce numéro? *voolay voo mahpuhlay suh newmayroa?*
Could you put me through to.../ extension..., please?	Voulez-vous me passer.../le poste...? *voolay voo muh pahsay…/luh post…?*
What's the charge per minute?	Quel est le prix à la minute? *kehl eh luh pree ah lah meenewt?*
Have there been any calls for me?	Quelqu'un m'a-t-il appelé? *kehlkuhn mah teel ahpuhlay?*

The conversation

Hello, this is...	Allô, ici... *ahloa, eesee…*
Who is this, please?	Qui est à l'appareil? *kee eh tah lahpahrehy?*
Is this...?	Je parle à...? *jhuh pahrl ah…?*
I'm sorry, I've dialled the wrong number	Pardon, je me suis trompé(e) de numéro *pahrdawn, jhuh muh swee trawnpay duh newmayroa.*

English	French	Pronunciation
I can't hear you	Je ne vous entends pas	*jhuh nuh voo zohntohn pah*
I'd like to speak to...	Je voudrais parler à...	*jhuh voodreh pahrlay ah...*
Is there anybody who speaks English?	Y a-t-il quelqu'un qui parle l'anglais?	*ee yah teel kehlkuhn kee pahrl lohngleh?*
Extension... please	Pouvez-vous me passer le poste...?	*poovay voo muh pahsay luh post...?*
Could you ask him/her to call me back?	Voulez-vous demander qu'il/qu'elle me rappelle?	*voolay voo duhmohnday keel/kehl muh rahpehl?*
My name's... My number's...	Mon nom est...Mon numéro est...	*mawn nawn eh...mawn newmayroa eh...*
Could you tell him/her I called?	Voulez-vous dire que j'ai appelé?	*voolay voo deer kuh jhay ahpuhlay?*
I'll call back tomorrow	Je rappellerai demain	*jhuh rahpehluhray duhmah*

French	English
On vous demande au téléphone	There's a phone call for you
Vous devez d'abord faire le zéro	You have to dial '0' first
Vous avez un instant?	One moment, please
Je n'obtiens pas de réponse	There's no answer
La ligne est occupée	The line's engaged
Vous voulez attendre?	Could you hold?
Je vous passe la communication	Putting you through
Vous vous êtes trompé de numéro	You've got the wrong number
Il/elle n'est pas ici en ce moment	He's/she's not here right now
Vous pouvez le/la rappeler à...	He'll/she'll be back...
C'est le répondeur automatique de...	This is the answering machine of...

● **Opening times:** Tuesday to Saturday 8/9am–1pm and 2.30–7pm. On Mondays shops are closed in the morning or for the entire day. On Sunday mornings grocers and bakers are usually open, and markets are open until 1pm. Supermarkets and department stores in nearly all cities are open until 8pm once a week. Chemists display the list of *pharmacies de garde* (those open on Sundays and after hours), but you may be charged double in some cities. You may be asked to pay in advance for shoe repairs and dry cleaning.

10.1 Shopping conversations

Where can I get...?	Dans quel magasin puis-je acheter...?
	dohn kehl mahgahzahn pwee jhahshtay...?
When does this shop open?	A quelle heure ouvre ce magasin?
	ah kehl uhr oovr suh mahgahzahn?
Could you tell me where the...department is?	Pouvez-vous m'indiquer le rayon de...?
	poovay voo mahndeekay luh rayawn duh...?
Could you help me, please? I'm looking for...	Pouvez-vous m'aider? Je cherche...
	poovay voo mayday? jhuh shehrsh...
Do you sell English/ American newspapers?	Vendez-vous des journaux anglais/américains?
	vohnday voo day jhoornoa ohngleh/ahmayreekahn?

On s'occupe de vous?	Are you being served?

No, I'd like...	Non. J'aimerais...
	nawn. jhehmuhreh...
I'm just looking, if that's all right	Je jette un coup d'oeil, si c'est permis
	jhuh jheht uhn koo duhy, see seh pehrmee

antiquités antiques
appareils
électriques
electrical appliances
bijoutier jeweller
blanchisserie
laundry
boucherie butcher
boulangerie bakery
centre commercial
shopping centre
charcuterie
delicatessen
coiffeur
(femmes/hommes)
hairdresser
(women/men)
cordonnier cobbler
crémerie dairy
épicerie grocery
store
fleuriste florist
fruits et légumes
greengrocer
galerie marchande
shopping arcade
grand magasin
department store

laverie automatique
launderette
librairie bookshop
magasin shop
magasin
d'ameublement
furniture shop
magasin
d'appareils
photographiques
camera shop
magasin de
bicyclettes bicycle
shop
magasin de
bricolage DIY-store
magasin de jouets
toy shop
magasin de disques
record shop
magasin de
souvenirs souvenir
shop
magasin de sport
sports shop
magasin de vins et
spiritueux off-
licence

magasin diététique
health food shop
marché market
marché aux puces
fleamarket
mercerie draper
pâtisserie cake shop
pharmacie chemist
poissonnerie
fishmonger
produits ménagers/
droguerie
household goods
quincaillerie
hardware shop
réparateur de
bicyclettes bicycle
repairs
salon de beauté
beauty parlour
salon de dégustation
de glaces ice-
cream parlour
supermarché
supermarket
tabac tobacconist
teinturerie dry-
cleaner

Vous désirez autre chose?   Anything else?

Yes, I'd also like... _____   Oui, donnez-moi aussi...
                               wee, donay mwah oasee...

No, thank you _____ That's all	**Non, je vous remercie. Ce sera tout** *nawn, jhuh voo ruhmehrsee. suh suhrah too*
Could you show me...? _	**Pouvez-vous me montrer...?** *poovay voo muh mawntray…?*
I'd prefer... _____	**Je préfère...** *jhuh prayfehr…*
This is not what I'm ____ looking for	**Ce n'est pas ce que je cherche** *suh neh pah suh kuh jhuh shehrsh*
Thank you. I'll keep ____ looking	**Merci. Je chercherai ailleurs** *mehrsee. jhuh shehrshuhray ahyuhr*
Do you have _____ something...?	**Vous n'avez pas quelque chose de...?** *voo nahvay pah kehlkuh shoaz duh…?*
– less expensive?_____	**Vous n'avez pas quelque chose de moins cher?** *voo nahvay pah kehlkuh shoaz duh mwahn shehr?*
– something smaller? __	**Vous n'avez pas quelque chose de plus petit?** *voo nahvay pah kehlkuh shoaz duh plew puhtee?*
– something larger? ____	**Vous n'avez pas quelque chose de plus grand?** *voo nahvay pah kehlkuh shoaz duh plew grohn?*
I'll take this one _____	**Je prends celui-ci** *jhuh prohn suhlwee see*
Does it come with ____ instructions?	**Y a-t-il un mode d'emploi avec?** *ee yah teel uhn mod dohnplwah ahvehk?*
It's too expensive_____	**Je le trouve trop cher** *jhuh luh troov troa shehr*
I'll give you... _____	**Je vous offre...** *jhuh voo zofr…*
Could you keep this ___ for me? I'll come back for it later	**Voulez-vous me le mettre de côté? Je reviendrai le chercher tout à l'heure** *voolay voo muh luh mehtr duh koatay? jhuh ruhvyahndray luh shehrshay too tah luhr*

Je suis désolé, nous n'en avons pas	I'm sorry, we don't have that
Je suis désolé, le stock est épuisé	I'm sorry, we're sold out
Je suis désolé, ce ne sera pas livré avant...	I'm sorry, that won't be in until...
Vous pouvez payer à la caisse	You can pay at the cash desk
Nous n'acceptons pas les cartes de crédit	We don't accept credit cards
Nous n'acceptons pas les chèques de voyage	We don't accept traveller's cheques
Nous n'acceptons pas les devises étrangères	We don't accept foreign currency

Have you got a bag for me, please? **Vous avez un sac?**
voo zahvay uhn sahk?

Could you giftwrap it, please? **Vous pouvez l'emballer dans un papier cadeau?**
voo poovay lohnbahlay dohn zuhn pahpyay kahdoa?

10.2 Food

I'd like a hundred grams of..., please **Je voudrais cent grammes de...**
jhuh voodreh sohn grahm duh...

– five hundred grams/ half a kilo of... **Je voudrais une livre de...**
jhuh voodreh zewn leevr duh...

– a kilo of... **Je voudrais un kilo de...**
jhuh voodreh zuhn keeloa duh...

Could you...it for me, please? **Vous voulez me le...?**
voo voolay muh luh...?

Could you slice it/ dice it for me, please?	Vous voulez me le couper en tranches/morceaux?
	voo voolay muh luh koopay ohn trohnsh/mohrsoa?
Could you grate it for me, please?	Vous voulez me le râper?
	voo voolay muh luh rahpay?
Can I order it?	Puis-je le commander?
	pwee jhuh luh komohnday?
I'll pick it up tomorrow/ at...	Je viendrai le chercher demain/à...heures
	jhuh vyahndray luh shehrshay duhmahn/ah…uhr
Can you eat/drink this?	Est-ce mangeable/buvable?
	ehs mohnjhahbl/bewvahbl?
What's in it?	Qu'y a-t-il dedans?
	kee yah teel duhdohn?

10.3 Clothing and shoes

I saw something in the window. Shall I point it out?	J'ai vu quelque chose dans la vitrine. Je vous le montre?
	jhay vew kehlkuh shoaz dohn lah veetreen. jhuh voo lah mawntr?
I'd like something to go with this	J'aimerais quelque chose pour aller avec ceci
	jhehmuhreh kehlkuh shoaz poor ahlay ahvehk suhsee
Do you have shoes to match this?	Avez-vous des chaussures de la même couleur que ça?
	ahvay voo day shoasewr duh lah mehm kooluhr kuh sah?
I'm a size...in the UK	Je fais du...au Royaume-Uni
	jhuh feh dew…oa rwahyoam ewnee
Can I try this on?	Puis-je l'essayer?
	pwee jhuh lehsayay?
Where's the fitting room?	Où est la cabine d'essayage?
	oo eh lah kahbeen dehsayahjh?

Ne pas repasser	Nettoyage à sec	Étendre humide
Do not iron	Dry clean	Drip dry
Laver à la main	Ne pas essorer	Laver à la machine
Hand wash	Do not spin dry	Machine wash

It doesn't fit _____ Cela ne me va pas
suhlah nuh muh vah pah

This is the right size____ C'est la bonne taille
seh lah bon tahy

It doesn't suit me _____ Cela ne me convient pas
suhlah nuh muh kawnvyahn pah

Do you have this in...? _ L'avez-vous aussi en...?
lahvay voo zoasee ohn...?

The heel's too high/low_ Je trouve le talon trop haut/bas
jhuh troov luh tahlawn troa oa/bah

Is this/are these _____ Est-ce/sont-elles en cuir?
  genuine leather? *eh suh/sawn tehl ohn kweer?*

I'm looking for a... _____ Je cherche un...pour un bébé/enfant
  for a...-year-old   de...ans
  baby/child *jhuh shehrsh uhn...poor uhn*
  baybay/ohnhfohn duh...ohn

I'd like a... ... _____ J'aurais aimé un...de...
jhoareh zaymay uhn... duh...

– silk _____ J'aurais aimé un...de soie
jhoareh zaymay uhn...duh swah

– cotton _____ J'aurais aimé un...de coton
jhoareh zaymay uhn...duh koatawn

– woollen _____ J'aurais aimé un...de laine
jhoareh zaymay uhn...duh lehn

– linen_____ J'aurais aimé un...de lin
jhoareh zaymay uhn...duh lahn

What temperature _____ A quelle température puis-je le laver?
  can I wash it at? *ah kehl tohnpayrahtewr pwee jhuh luh*
  lahvay?

Will it shrink in the _____ Cela rétrécit au lavage?
  wash? *suhlah raytraysee oa lahvahjh?*

At the cobbler

Could you mend these shoes?	**Pouvez-vous réparer ces chaussures?**
	poovay voo raypahray say shoasewr?
Could you put new soles/heels on these?	**Pouvez-vous y mettre de nouvelles semelles/nouveaux talons?**
	poovay voo zee mehtr duh noovehl suhmehl/noovoa tahlawn?
When will they be ready?	**Quand seront-elles prêtes?**
	kohn suhrawn tehl preht?
I'd like..., please	**Je voudrais...**
	jhuh voodreh...
– a tin of shoe polish	**Je voudrais une boîte de cirage**
	jhuh voodreh zewn bwaht duh seerahjh
– a pair of shoelaces	**Je voudrais une paire de lacets**
	jhuh voodreh zewn pehr duh lahseh

10.4 Photographs and video

I'd like a film for this camera, please	**Je voudrais un rouleau de pellicules pour cet appareil**
	jhuh voodreh zuhn rooloa duh payleekewl poor seht ahpahrehy
– a 126 cartridge	**Je voudrais une cartouche de cent vingt-six**
	jhuh voodreh zewn kahrtoosh duh sohn vahn sees
– a slide film	**Je voudrais un rouleau de pellicules pour diapositives**
	jhuh voodreh zuhn rooloa duh payleekewl poor deeahpoaseeteev
– a film	**Je voudrais un rouleau de pellicules**
	jhuh voodreh zuhn rooloa duh payleekewl
– a videotape	**Je voudrais une vidéocassette**
	jhuh voodreh zewn veedayoakahseht

colour/black and white ___	couleur/noir et blanc
	kooluhr/nwahr ay blohn
super eight _____	super huit mm
	sewpehr wee meeleemehtr
12/24/36 exposures____	douze/vingt-quatre/trente-six poses
	dooz/vahn kahtr/trohnt see poaz
ASA/DIN number _____	nombre d'ASA/DIN
	nohnbr dahzah/deen
daylight film_____	film pour la lumière du jour
	feelm poor lah lewmyehr dew joor
film for artificial light ___	film pour la lumière artificielle
	feelm poor lah lewmyehr ahrteefeesyehl

Problems

Could you load the ____ film for me, please?	Voulez-vous mettre le film dans l'appareil?
	voolay voo mehtr luh feelm dohn lahpahrehy?
Could you take the film_ out for me, please?	Voulez-vous enlever le film de l'appareil-photo?
	voolay voo zohnluhvay luh feelm duh lahpahrehy foatoa?
Should I replace _____ the batteries?	Dois-je changer les piles?
	dwah jhuh shohnjhay lay peel?
Could you have a look _ at my camera, please? It's not working	Voulez-vous jeter un coup d'oeil à mon appareil-photo? Il ne marche plus
	voolay voo jhuhtay uhn koo duhy ah mawn nahpahrehy foatoa? eel nuh mahrsh plew
The...is broken _____	Le...est cassé
	luh...eh kahssay
The film's jammed _____	La pellicule est bloquée
	lah payleekewl eh blokay
The film's broken _____	La pellicule est cassée
	lah payleekewl eh kahssay
The flash isn't working _	Le flash ne marche pas
	luh flahsh nuh mahrsh pah

Processing and prints

I'd like to have this film developed/printed, please	Je voudrais faire développer/tirer ce film _jhuh voodreh fehr dayvuhlopay/teeray suh feelm_
I'd like...prints from ____ each negative	Je voudrais...tirages de chaque négatif _jhuh voodreh...teerahjh duh shahk naygahteef_
glossy/mat_____	brillant/mat _breeyohn/maht_
6x9 _____	six sur neuf _sees sewr nuhf_
I'd like to re-order _____ these photos	Je veux faire refaire cette photo _jhuh vuh fehr ruhfehr seht foatoa_
I'd like to have this_____ photo enlarged	Je veux faire agrandir cette photo _jhuh vuh fehr ahgrohndeer seht foatoa_
How much is_____ processing?	Combien coûte le développement? _kawnbyahn koot luh dayvuhlopmohn?_
– printing _____	Combien coûte le tirage? _kawnbyahn koot luh teerahjh?_
– to re-order _____	Combien coûte la commande supplémentaire? _kawnbyahn koot lah komohnd sewplaymohntehr?_
– the enlargement _____	Combien coûte l'agrandissement? _kawnbyahn koot lahgrohndeesmohn?_
When will they _____ be ready?	Quand seront-elles prêtes? _kohn suhrawn tehl preht?_

10.5 At the hairdresser's

Do I have to make an ____ appointment?	Dois-je prendre un rendez-vous? _dwah jhuh prohndr uhn rohnday voo?_
Can I come in straight____ away?	Pouvez-vous vous occuper de moi immédiatement? _poovay voo voo zokewpay duh mwah eemaydyahtmohn?_

How long will I have to wait?	Combien de temps dois-je attendre?
	kawnbyahn duh tohn dwah jhahtohndr?
I'd like a shampoo/ haircut	Je veux me faire laver/couper les cheveux
	jhuh vuh muh fehr lahvay/koopay lay shuhvuh
I'd like a shampoo for oily/dry hair, please	Je voudrais un shampooing pour cheveux gras/secs
	jhuh voodreh zuhn shohnpwahn poor shuhvuh grah/sehk
an anti-dandruff shampoo	Je voudrais un shampooing anti-pelliculaire
	jhuh voodreh zuhn shohnpwahn ohnteepayleekewlehr
– a shampoo for permed/coloured hair	Je voudrais un shampooing pour cheveux permanentés/colorés
	jhuh voodreh zuhn shohnpwahn poor shuhvuh pehrmahnohntay/kohlohray
– a colour rinse shampoo	Je voudrais un shampooing colorant
	jhuh voodreh zuhn shohnpwahn kolorohn
– a shampoo with conditioner	Je voudrais un shampoing avec un soin traitant
	jhuh voodreh zuhn shohnpwahn ahvehk uhn swahn trehtohn
– highlights	Je voudrais me faire faire des mèches
	jhuh voodreh muh fehr fehr day mehsh
Do you have a colour chart, please?	Avez-vous une carte de coloration s'il vous plaît?
	ahvay voo zewn kahrt duh kolorahsyawn seel voo pleh?
I want to keep it the same colour	Je veux garder la même couleur
	jhuh vuh gahrday lah mehm kooluhr
I'd like it darker/lighter	Je les veux plus sombres/clairs
	jhuh lay vuh plew sawmbr/klehr

I'd like/I don't want ____ hairspray	**Je veux de la/ne veux pas de laque** *jhuh vuh duh la/nuh vuh pah duh lahk*
– gel _____	**Je veux du/ne veux pas de gel** *jhuh vuh dew/ nuh vuh pah duh jhehl*
– lotion _____	**Je veux de la/ne veux pas de lotion** *jhuh vuh duh lah/nuh vuh pah duh loasyawn*
I'd like a short fringe ___	**Je veux ma frange courte** *jhuh vuh mah frohnjh koort*
Not too short at the ____ back	**Je ne veux pas la nuque trop courte** *jhuh nuh vuh pah lah newk troa koort*
Not too long here_____	**Ici je ne les veux pas trop longs** *eesee jhuh nuh lay vuh pah troa lawn*
I'd like/I don't want ____ (many) curls	**Je (ne) veux (pas) être (trop) frisée** *jhuh (nuh) vuh (pah) ehtr (troa) freezay*
It needs a little/_____ a lot taken off	**Il faut en enlever une petite/grande quantité** *eel foa ohn nohnluhvay ewn puhteet/grohnd kohnteetay*
I want a completely ____ different style	**Je veux une toute autre coupe** *jhuh vuh zewn toot oatr koop*
I'd like it like..._____	**Je veux mes cheveux comme...** *jhuh vuh may shuhvuh kom...*
– the same as that lady's _____	**Je veux la même coiffure que cette femme** *jhuh vuh lah mehm kwahfewr kuh seht fahm*
– the same as in this ___ photo	**Je veux la même coiffure que sur cette photo** *jhuh vuh lah mehm kwahfewr kuh sewr seht foatoa*
Could you put the ____ drier up/down a bit?	**Pouvez-vous mettre le casque plus haut/plus bas?** *poovay voo mehtr luh kahsk plew oa/plew bah?*
I'd like a facial_____	**J'aimerais un masque de beauté** *jhehmuhreh zuhn mahsk duh boatay*

Quelle coupe de cheveux désirez-vous?	How do you want it cut?
Quelle coiffure désirez-vous?	What style did you have in mind?
Quelle couleur désirez-vous?	What colour do you want it?
Est-ce la bonne température?	Is the temperature all right for you?
Voulez-vous lire quelque chose?	Would you like something to read?
Voulez-vous boire quelque chose?	Would you like a drink?
C'est ce que vous vouliez?	Is this what you had in mind?

– a manicure _____	J'aimerais qu'on me fasse les ongles *jhehmuhreh kawn muh fahs lay zawngl*
– a massage _____	J'aimerais un massage *jhehmuhreh zuhn mahsahjh*
Could you trim _____ my fringe?	Pouvez-vous égaliser ma frange? *poovay voo zaygahleezay mah frohnjh?*
– my beard? _____	Pouvez-vous égaliser ma barbe? *poovay voo zaygahleezay mah bahrb?*
– my moustache? _____	Pouvez-vous égaliser ma moustache? *poovay voo zaygahleezay mah moostahsh?*
I'd like a shave, please _	Pouvez-vous me raser s'il vous plaît? *poovay voo muh rahzay seel voo pleh?*
I'd like a wet shave, _____ please	Je veux être rasé au rasoir à main *jhuh vuh zehtr rahzay oa rahzwahr ah mahn*

11

At the Tourist Information Centre

11.1 Places of interest

Where's the Tourist Information, please?	Où est l'office de tourisme? *oo eh lofees duh tooreesm?*
Do you have a city map?	Avez-vous un plan de la ville? *ahvay voo zuhn plohn duh lah veel?*
Where is the museum?	Où est le musée? *oo eh luh mewzay?*
Where can I find a church?	Où puis-je trouver une église? *oo pwee jhuh troovay ewn aygleez?*
Could you give me some information about...?	Pouvez-vous me renseigner sur...? *poovay voo muh rohnsehnyay sewr...?*
How much is that?	Combien ça coûte? *kawnbyahn sah koot?*
What are the main places of interest?	Quelles sont les curiosités les plus importantes? *kehl sawn lay kewryoseetay lay plewz ahnportohnt?*
Could you point them out on the map?	Pouvez-vous les indiquer sur la carte? *poovay voo lay zahndeekay sewr lah kahrt?*
What do you recommend?	Que nous conseillez-vous? *kuh noo kawnsehyay voo?*
We'll be here for a few hours	Nous restons ici quelques heures. *noo rehstawn zeesee kehlkuh zuhr.*
– a day	Nous restons ici une journée. *noo rehstawn zeesee ewn jhoornay.*
– a week	Nous restons ici une semaine. *noo rehstawn zeesee ewn suhmehn.*
We're interested in...	Nous sommes intéressés par... *noo som zahntayrehsay pahr...*
Is there a scenic walk around the city?	Pouvons-nous faire une promenade en ville? *poovawn noo fehr ewn promuhnahd ohn veel?*

How long does it take?_	**Combien de temps dure-t-elle?**
	kawnbyahn duh tohn dewr tehl?
Where does it _____ start/end?	**Où est le point de départ/d'arrivée?**
	oo eh luh pwahn duh daypahr/dahreevay?
Are there any boat _____ cruises here?	**Y a-t-il des bateaux-mouches?**
	ee yah teel day bahtoa moosh?
Where can we board?__	**Où pouvons-nous embarquer?**
	oo poovawn noo zohnbahrkay?
Are there any bus_____ tours?	**Y a-t-il des promenades en bus?**
	ee yah teel day promuhnahd ohn bews?
Where do we get on? __	**Où devons-nous monter?**
	oo devawn noo mawntay?
Is there a guide who ___ speaks English?	**Y a-t-il un guide qui parle l'anglais?**
	ee yah teel uhn gueed kee pahrl lohngleh?
What trips can we take_ around the area?	**Quelles promenades peut-on faire dans la région?**
	kehl promuhnahd puh tawn fehr dohn lah rayjhyawn?
Are there any_____ excursions?	**Y a-t-il des excursions?**
	ee yah teel day zehxkewrsyawn?
Where do they go to? __	**Où vont-elles?**
	oo vawn tehl?
We'd like to go to... ____	**Nous voulons aller à...**
	noo voolawn zahlay ah...
How long is the trip? ___	**Combien de temps dure l'excursion?**
	kawnbyahn duh tohn dewr lehxkewrsyawn?
How long do we_____ stay in...?	**Combien de temps restons-nous à...?**
	kawnbyahn duh tohn rehstawn noo zah...?
Are there any guided ___ tours?	**Y a-t-il des visites guidées?**
	ee yah teel day veezeet gueeday?
How much free time ___ will we have there?	**Combien de temps avons-nous de libre?**
	kawnbyahn duh tohn ahvawn noo duh leebr?
We want to go hiking___	**Nous voulons faire une randonnée**
	noo voolawn fehr ewn rohndonay
Can we hire a guide? __	**Pouvons-nous prendre un guide?**
	poovawn noo prohndr uhn gueed?

Can I book mountain huts?	**Puis-je réserver un refuge?** *pwee jhuh rayzehrvay uhn ruhfewjhuh?*
What time does... open/close?	**A quelle heure ouvre/ferme...?** *ah kehl uhr oovr/fehrm...?*
What days is...open/ closed?	**Quels sont les jours d'ouverture/de fermeture de...?** *kehl sawn lay jhoor doovehrtewr/duh fehrmuhtewr duh...?*
What's the admission price?	**Quel est le prix d'entrée?** *kehl eh luh pree dohntray?*
Is there a group discount?	**Y a-t-il une réduction pour les groupes?** *ee yah teel ewn raydewksyawn poor lay groop?*
Is there a child discount?	**Y a-t-il une réduction pour les enfants?** *ee yah teel ewn raydewksyawn poor lay zohnfohn?*
Is there a discount for pensioners?	**Y a-t-il une réduction pour les personnes de plus de soixante-cinq ans?** *ee yah teel ewn raydewksyawn poor lay pehrson duh plew duh swahssohnt sahnk ohn?*
Can I take (flash) photos/can I film here?	**M'est-il permis de prendre des photos(avec flash)/filmer ici?** *meh teel pehrmee duh prohndr day foatoa(ahvehk flahsh)/feelmay eesee?*
Do you have any postcards of...?	**Vendez-vous des cartes postales de...?** *vohnday voo day kahrt postahl duh...?*
Do you have an English...?	**Avez-vous un...en anglais?** *ahvay voo zuhn...ohn nohngleh?*
– an English catalogue?	**Avez-vous un catalogue en anglais?** *ahvay voo zuhn kahtahlog ohn nohngleh?*
– an English programme?	**Avez-vous un programme en anglais?** *ahvay voo zuhn prograhm ohn nohngleh?*
– an English brochure?	**Avez-vous une brochure en anglais?** *ahvay voo zewn broshewr ohn nohngleh?*

11.2 Going out

● **In French theatres** you are usually shown to your seat by an usherette from whom you can buy a programme. It is customary to tip. At the cinema most films are dubbed *(version française)*. In large cities subtitled versions are often screened, advertised as *version originale* or *V.O.* If the publicity does not mention *V.O.*, the film will be dubbed. *L'Officiel des spectacles* (an entertainment guide) can be obtained from newspaper kiosks

Do you have this week's/month's entertainment guide?	Avez-vous le journal des spectacles de cette semaine/de ce mois? *ahvay voo luh jhoornal day spehktahkl duh seht suhmehn/duh suh mwah?*
What's on tonight?	Que peut-on faire ce soir? *kuh puh tawn fehr suh swahr?*
We want to go to...	Nous voulons aller au... *noo voolawn zahlay oa...*
Which films are showing?	Quels films passe-t-on? *kehl feelm pah stawn?*
What sort of film is that?	Qu'est-ce que c'est comme film? *kehs kuh seh kom feelm?*
suitable for all ages	pour tous les âges *poor too lay zahjh*
not suitable for children under 12/16 years	pour les plus de douze ans/seize ans *poor lay plew duh dooz ohn/sehz ohn*
original version	version originale *vehrsyawn oreejheenahl*
subtitled	sous-titré *soo teetray*
dubbed	doublé *dooblay*
Is it a continuous showing?	Est-ce un spectacle permanent? *ehs uhn spehktahkl pehrmahnohn?*

What's on at...? _____	**Qu'y a-t-il au...?** *kee yah teel oa...?*
– the theatre? _____	**Qu'y a-t-il au théâtre?** *kee yah teel oa tayahtr?*
– the concert hall? _____	**Qu'y a-t-il à la salle des concerts?** *kee yah teel ah lah sahl day kawnsehr?*
– the opera? _____	**Qu'y a-t-il à l'opéra?** *kee yah teel ah loapayrah?*
Where can I find a _____ gooddisco around here?	**Où se trouve une bonne disco par ici?** *oo suh troov ewn bon deeskoa pahr eesee?*
Is it members only? ____	**Exige-t-on une carte de membre?** *ehgzeejh-tawn ewn kahrt duh mohnbr?*
Where can I find a _____ good nightclub around here?	**Où se trouve une bonne boîte de nuit par ici?** *oo suh troov ewn bon bwaht duh nwee pahr eesee?*
Is it evening wear _____ only?	**La tenue de soirée, est-elle obligatoire?** *lah tuhnew duh swahray, eh tehl obleegahtwahr?*
Should I/we dress up? _	**La tenue de soirée, est-elle souhaitée?** *lah tuhnew duh swahray ehtehl sooehtay?*
What time does the _____ show start?	**A quelle heure commence la représentation?** *ah kehl uhr komohns lah ruhprayzohntahsyawn?*
When's the next _____ soccer match?	**Quand est le prochain match de football?** *kohn teh luh proshahn mahtch duh footbohl?*
Who's playing? _____	**Qui joue contre qui?** *kee jhoo kawntr kee?*
I'd like an escort for____ tonight. Could you arrange that for me?	**Je veux une hôtesse pour ce soir. Pouvez-vous arranger ça?** *jhuh vuh zewn oatehs poor suh swahr. poovay voo zahrohnjhay sah?*

11.3 Booking tickets

Could you book some___ tickets for us?	Pouvez-vous nous faire une réservation? *poovay voo noo fehr ewn rayzehrvahsyawn?*
We'd like to book... ____ seats/a table...	Nous voulons...places/une table... *noo voolawn...plahs/ewn tahbl...*
– in the stalls_____	Nous voulons...places à l'orchestre. *noo voolawn...plahs ah lorkehstr*
– on the balcony_____	Nous voulons...places au balcon. *noo voolawn...plahs oa bahlkawn*
– box seats _____	Nous voulons...places dans les loges. *noo voolawn...plahs dohn lay lojh*
– a table at the front ___	Nous voulons...une table à l'avant. *noo voolawn...ewn tahbl ah lahvohn*
– in the middle _____	Nous voulons...places au milieu. *noo voolawn...plahs oa meelyuh*
– at the back_____	Nous voulons...places à l'arrière. *noo voolawn...plahs ah lahryehr*
Could I book... _____ seats for the...o'clock performance?	Puis-je réserver...places pour la représentation de...heures? *pwee jhuh rayzehrvay...plahs poor lah ruhprayzohntahsyawn duh...uhr?*
Are there any seats left _ for tonight?	Reste-t-il encore des places pour ce soir? *rehst-uh-teel ohnkor day plahs poor suh swahr?*
How much is a ticket? _	Combien coûte un billet? *kawnbyahn koot uhn beeyeh?*
When can I pick the____ tickets up?	Quand puis-je venir chercher les billets? *kohn pwee jhuh vuhneer shehrshay lay beeyeh?*
I've got a reservation___	J'ai réservé *jhay rayzehrvay*
My name's... _____	Mon nom est... *mawn nawn eh...*

11

11

At the Tourist Information Centre

Vous voulez réserver pour quelle représentation?	Which performance do you want to book for?
Où voulez-vous vous asseoir?	Where would you like to sit?
Tout est vendu	Everything's sold out
Il ne reste que des places debout	We've only got standing spaces left
Il ne reste que des places au balcon	We've only got balcony seats left
Il ne reste que des places au poulailler	We've only got seats left in the gallery
Il ne reste que des places d'orchestre	We've only got stalls seats left
Il ne reste que des places à l'avant	We've only got seats left at the front
Il ne reste que des places à l'arrière	We've only got seats left at the back
Combien de places voulez-vous?	How many seats would you like?
Vous devez venir chercher les billets avant...heures	You'll have to pick up the tickets before...o'clock
Puis-je voir vos billets?	Tickets, please
Voici votre place	This is your seat
Vous n'êtes pas aux bonnes places	You're in the wrong seats

12.1 Sporting questions

Where can we... _____ around here?	Où pouvons-nous...?
	oo poovawn noo...?
Is there a... _____ around here?	Y a-t-il un...dans les environs?
	ee yah teel uhn...dohn lay zohnveerawn?
Can I hire a...here? ____	Puis-je louer un...ici?
	pwee jhuh looay uhn...eesee?
Can I take...lessons? ___	Puis-je prendre des cours de...?
	pwee jhuh prohndr day koor duh...?
How much is that per __ hour/per day/a turn?	Quel est le prix à l'heure/à la journée/à chaque fois?
	kehl eh luh pree ah luhr/ah lah jhoornay/ah shahk fwah?
Do I need a permit_____ for that?	A-t-on besoin d'un permis?
	ah tawn buhzwahn duhn pehrmee?
Where can I get _____ the permit?	Où puis-je obtenir le permis?
	oo pwee jhuh obtuhneer luh pehrmee?

12.2 By the waterfront

Is it a long way to_____ the sea still?	La mer, est-elle encore loin?
	lah mehr eh tehl ohnkor lwahn?
Is there a...around _____ here?	Y a-t-il un...dans les environs?
	ee yah teel uhn...dohn lay zohnveerawn?
– a public swimming ___ pool	Y a-t-il une piscine dans les environs?
	ee yah teel ewn peeseen dohn lay zohnveerawn?
– a sandy beach_____	Y a-t-il une plage de sable dans les environs?
	ee yah teel ewn plahjh duh sahbl dohn lay zohnveerawn?

– a nudist beach	Y a-t-il une plage pour nudistes dans les environs?
	ee yah teel ewn plahjh poor newdeest dohn lay zohnveerawn?
– mooring	Y a-t-il un embarcadère pour les bateaux dans les environs?
	ee yah teel uhn nohnbahrkahdehr poor lay bahtoa dohn lay zohnveerawn?
Are there any rocks here?	Y a-t-il aussi des rochers ici?
	ee yah teel oasee day roshay eesee?
When's high/low tide?	Quand est la marée haute/basse?
	kohn teh lah mahray oat/bahs?
What's the water temperature?	Quelle est la température de l'eau?
	kehl eh lah tohnpayratewr duh loa?
Is it (very) deep here?	Est-ce (très) profond ici?
	ehs (treh) proafawn eesee?
Can you stand here?	A-t-on pied ici?
	ah tawn pyay eesee?
Is it safe to swim here?	Peut-on nager en sécurité ici?
	puh tawn nahjhay ohn saykewreetay eesee?
Are there any currents?	Y a-t-il des courants?
	ee yah teel day koorohn?
Are there any rapids/ waterfalls in this river?	Est-ce que cette rivière a des courants rapides/des chutes d'eau?
	ehs kuh seht reevyehr ah day koorohn rahpeed/day shewt doa?
What does that flag/ buoy mean?	Que signifie ce drapeau/cette bouée là-bas?
	kuh seenyeefee suh drahpoa/seht booway lah bah?

Danger	**Pêche interdite**	**Baignade interdite**
Danger	No fishing	No swimming
Pêche	**Surf interdit**	**Seulement avec**
Fishing water	No surfing	**permis** Permits only

Is there a life guard ____ on duty here?	Y a-t-il un maître nageur qui surveille?
	ee yah teel uhn mehtr nahjhuhr kee sewrvehy?
Are dogs allowed _____ here?	Les chiens sont admis ici?
	lay shyahn sawn tahdmee eesee?
Is camping on the ____ beach allowed?	Peut-on camper sur la plage?
	puh tawn kohnpay sewr lah plahjh?
Are we allowed to ____ build a fire here?	Peut-on faire un feu ici?
	puh tawn fehr uhn fuh eesee?

12.3 In the snow

Can I take ski lessons __ here?	Puis-je prendre des leçons de ski?
	pwee jhuh prohndr day luhsawn duh skee?
for beginners/ _____ advanced	pour débutants/initiés
	poor daybewtohn/eeneesyay
How large are the_____ groups?	Quelle est la taille des groupes?
	kehl eh lah tahy day groop?
What language are_____ the classes in?	En quelle langue donne-t-on les leçons de ski?
	ohn kehl lohng don tawn lay luhsawn duh skee?
I'd like a lift pass, _____ please	Je voudrais un abonnement pour les remontées mécaniques.
	jhuh voodreh zuhn nahbonmohn poor lay ruhmawntay maykahneek
Must I give you a _____ passport photo?	Dois-je donner une photo d'identité?
	dwah jhuh donay ewn foatoa deedohnteetay?
Where can I have a ____ passport photo taken?	Où puis-je faire faire une photo d'identité?
	oo pwee jhuh fehr fehr ewn foatoa deedohnteetay?

Where are the _____ beginners' slopes?	Où sont les pistes de ski pour débutants?
	oo sawn lay peest duh skee poor daybewtohn?
Are there any runs for __ cross-country skiing?	Y a-t-il des pistes de ski de fond dans les environs?
	ee yah teel day peest duh skee duh fawn dohn lay zohnveerawn?
Have the cross- _____ country runs been marked?	Les pistes de ski de fond, sont-elles indiquées?
	lay peest duh skee duh fawn, sawn tehl ahndeekay?
Are the...in operation?__	Est-ce que les...marchent?
	ehs kuh lay...mahrsh?
– the ski lifts _____	Est-ce que les remontées mécaniques marchent?
	ehs kuh lay ruhmawntay maykahneek mahrsh?
– the chair lifts _____	Est-ce que les télésièges marchent?
	ehs kuh lay taylaysyehjh mahrsh?
Are the slopes usable? _	Est-ce que les pistes sont ouvertes?
	ehs kuh lay peest sawn toovehrt?
Are the cross-country __ runs usable?	Est-ce que les pistes de ski de fond sont ouvertes?
	ehs kuh lay peest duh skee duh fawn sawn toovehrt?

13.1 Call (fetch) the doctor

Could you call/fetch a __ doctor quickly, please?	Voulez-vous vite appeler/aller chercher un médecin s'il vous plaît?
	voolay voo veet ahpuhlay/ahlay shehrshay uhn maydsahn seel voo pleh?
When does the doctor _ have surgery?	Quand est-ce que le médecin reçoit?
	kohn tehs kuh luh maydsahn ruhswah?
When can the doctor___ come?	Quand est-ce que le médecin peut venir?
	kohn tehs kuh luh maydsahn puh vuhneer?
I'd like to make an _____ appointment to see the doctor	Pouvez-vous me prendre un rendez-vous chez le médecin?
	poovay voo muh prohndr uhn rohnday voo shay luh maydsahn?
I've got an _____ appointment to see the doctor at...	J'ai un rendez-vous chez le médecin à...heures
	jhay uhn rohnday voo shay luh maydsahn a...uhr
Which doctor/chemist__ has night/weekend duty?	Quel médecin/Quelle pharmacie est de garde cette nuit/ce week-end?
	kehl maydsahn/kehl fahrmahsee eh duh gahrd seht nwee/suh week-ehnd?

13.2 Patient's ailments

I don't feel well _____	Je ne me sens pas bien
	jhuh nuh muh sohn pah byahn
I'm dizzy_____	J'ai des vertiges
	jhay day vehrteejh
– ill_____	Je suis malade
	jhuh swee mahlahd
– sick _____	J'ai mal au coeur
	jhay mahl oa kuhr

I've got a cold _____ **Je suis enrhumé(e)**
jhuh swee zohnrewmay

It hurts here _____ **J'ai mal ici**
jhay mahl eesee

I've been throwing up __ **J'ai vomi**
jhay vomee

I've got... _____ **Je souffre de...**
jhuh soofr duh...

I'm running a _____ **J'ai de la fièvre**
temperature *jhayduh lah fyehvr*

I've been stung by _____ **J'ai été piqué(e) par une guêpe**
a wasp. *jhay aytay peekay pahr ewn gehp*

I've been stung by an __ **J'ai été piqué(e) par un insecte**
insect *jhay aytay peekay pahr uhn nahnsehkt*

I've been bitten by _____ **J'ai été mordu(e) par un chien**
a dog *jhay aytay mordew pahr uhn shyahn*

I've been stung by _____ **J'ai été piqué(e) par une méduse**
a jellyfish *jhay aytay peekay pahr ewn maydewz*

I've been bitten by _____ **J'ai été mordu(e) par un serpent**
a snake *jhay aytay mordew pahr uhn sehrpohn*

I've been bitten by _____ **J'ai été mordu(e) par un animal**
an animal *jhay aytay mordew pahr uhn nahneemahl*

I've cut myself _____ **Je me suis coupé(e)**
jhuh muh swee koopay

I've burned myself _____ **Je me suis brûlé(e)**
jhuh muh swee brewlay

I've grazed myself _____ **Je me suis égratigné(e)**
jhuh muh swee zaygrahteenyay

I've had a fall _____ **Je suis tombé(e)**
jhuh swee tawnbay

I've sprained my ankle _ **Je me suis foulé(e) la cheville**
jhuh muh swee foolay lah shuhveey

I've come for the _____ **Je viens pour la pilule du lendemain**
morning-after pill *jhuh vyahn poor lah peelewl dew
lohndmahn*

13.3 The consultation

Quels sont vos symptômes?	What seems to be the problem?
Depuis combien de temps avez-vous ces symptômes?	How long have you had these symptoms?
Avez-vous eu ces symptômes auparavant?	Have you had this trouble before?
Avez-vous de la fièvre?	How high is your temperature?
Déshabillez-vous s'il vous plaît?	Get undressed, please
Pouvez-vous vous mettre torse nu?	Strip to the waist, please
Vous pouvez vous déshabiller là-bas.	You can undress there
Pouvez-vous remonter la manche de votre bras gauche/droit?	Roll up your left/right sleeve, please
Allongez-vous ici	Lie down here, please
Ceci vous fait mal?	Does this hurt?
Aspirez et expirez profondément	Breathe deeply
Ouvrez la bouche	Open your mouth

Patient's medical history

I'm a diabetic _____	Je suis diabétique
jhuh swee dyahbayteek
I have a heart condition _____	Je suis cardiaque
jhuh swee kahrdyahk
I have asthma _____	J'ai de l'asthme
jhay duh lahsm
I'm allergic to... _____	Je suis allergique à...
jhuh swee zahlehrjheek ah...

I'm...months pregnant _	**Je suis enceinte de...mois**
	jhuh swee zohnsahnt duh...mwah
I'm on a diet_____	**Je suis au régime**
	jhuh swee zoa rayjheem
I'm on medication/the _ pill	**Je prends des médicaments/la pilule**
	jhuh prohn day maydeekahmohn/lah peelewl
I've had a heart attack _ once before	**J'ai déjà eu une crise cardiaque**
	jhay dayjhah ew ewn kreez kahrdyahk
I've had a(n)...operation	**J'ai été opéré(e) de...**
	jhay aytay oapayray duh...
I've been ill recently ___	**Je viens d'être malade**
	jhuh vyahn dehtr mahlahd
I've got an ulcer_____	**J'ai un ulcère à l'estomac**
	jhay uhn newlsehr ah lehstomah
I've got my period_____	**J'ai mes règles**
	jhay may rehgl

Avez-vous des allergies?	Do you have any allergies?
Prenez-vous des médicaments?	Are you on any medication?
Suivez-vous un régime?	Are you on any sort of diet?
Etes-vous enceinte?	Are you pregnant?
Etes-vous vacciné(e) contre le tétanos?	Have you had a tetanus vaccination?

The diagnosis

Is it contagious? _____	**Est-ce contagieux?**
	ehs kawntahjhyuh?
How long do I have to _ stay...?	**Combien de temps dois-je rester...?**
	kawnbyahn duh tohn dwah jhuh rehstay...?
– in bed_____	**Combien de temps dois-je rester au lit?**
	kawnbyahn duh tohn dwah jhuh rehstay oa lee?

Ce n'est rien de grave	It's nothing serious
Vous vous êtes cassé le/la...	Your...is broken
Vous vous êtes foulé le/la...	You've sprained your...
Vous vous êtes déchiré le/la...	You've got a torn...
Vous avez une inflammation	You've got an inflammation
Vous avez une crise d'appendicite	You've got appendicitis
Vous avez une bronchite	You've got bronchitis
Vous avez une maladie vénérienne	You've got a venereal disease
Vous avez une grippe	You've got the flu
Vous avez eu une crise cardiaque	You've had a heart attack
Vous avez une infection (virale/bactérielle)	You've got an infection (viral/bacterial)
Vous avez une pneumonie	You've got pneumonia
Vous avez un ulcère à l'estomac	You've got an ulcer
Vous vous êtes froissé un muscle	You've pulled a muscle

– in hospital___	Combien de temps dois-je rester à l'hôpital? *kawnbyahn duh tohn dwah jhuh rehstay ah loapeetahl?*
Do I have to go on a special diet?	Dois-je suivre un régime? *dwah jhuh sweevr uhn rayjheem?*
Am I allowed to travel? _	Puis-je voyager? *pwee jhuh vwahyahjhay?*
Can I make a new appointment?	Puis-je prendre un autre rendez-vous? *pwee jhuh prohndr uhn noatr rohnday voo?*

Vous avez une infection vaginale	You've got a vaginal infection
Vous avez une intoxication alimentaire	You've got food poisoning
Vous avez une insolation	You've got sunstroke
Vous êtes allergique à...	You're allergic to...
Vous êtes enceinte	You're pregnant
Je veux faire analyser votre sang/urine/vos selles	I'd like to have your blood/urine/stools tested
Il faut faire des points de suture	It needs stitching
Je vous envoie à un spécialiste/l'hôpital	I'm referring you to a specialist/sending you to hospital.
Il faut faire des radios	You'll need to have some x-rays taken
Voulez-vous reprendre place un petitinstant dans la salle d'attente?	Could you wait in the waiting room, please?
Il faut vous opérer	You'll need an operation

When do I have to ___ come back?	**Quand dois-je revenir?** _kohn dwah jhuh ruhvuhneer?_
I'll come back ___ tomorrow	**Je reviendrai demain** _jhuh ruhvyahndray duhmahn_

Vous devez revenir demain/dans...jours	Come back tomorrow/in...days' time

13.4 Medication and prescriptions

How do I take this _____ medicine?	Comment dois-je prendre ces médicaments?
	komohn dwah jhuh prohndr say maydeekahmohn?
How many capsules/___ drops/injections/ spoonfuls/ tablets each time?	Combien de capsules/gouttes/piqûres/ cuillères/comprimés à chaque fois?
	kawnbyahn duh kahpsewl/goot/peekewr/ kweeyehr/kawnpreemay ah shahk fwah?
How many times a _____ day?	Combien de fois par jour?
	kawnbyahn duh fwah pahr jhoor?
I've forgotten my _____ medication. At home I take...	J'ai oublié mes médicaments. A la maison je prends...
	jhay oobleeyay may maydeekahmohn. ah lah mehzawn jhuh prohn...
Could you make out a___ prescription for me?	Pouvez-vous me faire une ordonnance?
	poovay voo muh fehr ewn ordonohns?

---

avaler entièrement swallow whole	cuillerées (...à soupe/...à café) spoonfuls (tablespoons/ teaspoons)	pendant...jours for...days
avant chaque repas before meals		piqûres injections
capsules capsules	dissoudre dans l'eau dissolve in water	pommade ointment
la prise de ce médicament peut rendre dangereuse la conduite automobile this medication impairs your driving	enduire rub on	prendre take
	finir le traitement finish the course	toutes les...heures every...hours
	...fois par jour ...times a day	uniquement pour usage externe not for internal use
comprimés tablets	gouttes drops	

Je vous prescris un antibiotique/un sirop/un tranquillisant/un calmant — I'm prescribing antibiotics/a mixture/a tranquillizer/pain killer

Vous devez rester au calme — Have lots of rest

Vous ne devez pas sortir — Stay indoors

Vous devez rester au lit — Stay in bed

13.5 At the dentist's

Do you know a good dentist? — Connaissez-vous un bon dentiste?
konehsay voo zuhn bawn dohnteest?

Could you make a dentist's appointment for me? It's urgent — Pouvez-vous me prendre un rendez-vous chez le dentiste? C'est urgent
poovay voo muh prohndr uhn rohnday voo shay luh dohnteest? seh tewrjhohn

Can I come in today, please? — Puis-je venir aujourd'hui s'il vous plaît?
pwee jhuh vuhneer oajhoordwee seel voo pleh?

I have (terrible) toothache — J'ai une rage de dents/un mal de dents(épouvantable)
jhay ewn rahjh duh dohn/uhn mahl duh dohn (aypoovohntahbl)

Could you prescribe/give me a painkiller? — Pouvez-vous me prescrire/donner un calmant?
poovay voo muh prehskreer/donay uhn kahlmohn?

A piece of my tooth has broken off — Ma dent s'est cassée
mah dohn seh kahssay

My filling's come out — Mon plombage est parti
mawn plawnbahjh eh pahrtee

I've got a broken crown — Ma couronne est cassée
mah kooron eh kahssay

151

I'd like/I don't want a___ local anaesthetic	Je (ne) veux (pas) une anesthésie locale *jhuh (nuh) vuh (paz) ewn ahnehstayzee lokahl*
Can you do a _____ makeshift repair job?	Pouvez-vous me soigner de façon provisoire? *poovay voo muh swahnyay duh fahsawn proveezwahr?*
I don't want this tooth__ pulled	Je ne veux pas que cette dent soit arrachée *jhuh nuh vuh pah kuh seht dohn swaht ahrahshay*
My dentures are _____ broken. Can you fix them?	Mon dentier est cassé. Pouvez-vous le réparer? *mawn dohntyay eh kahssay. poovay voo luh raypahray?*

Quelle dent/molaire vous fait mal?	Which tooth hurts?
Vous avez un abcès	You've got an abscess
Je dois faire une dévitalisation	I'll have to do a root canal
Je vais vous faire une anesthésie locale	I'm giving you a local anaesthetic
Je dois plomber/extraire/polir cette dent	I'll have to fill/pull/file this tooth
Je dois utiliser la roulette	I'll have to drill
Ouvrez bien la bouche	Open your mouth
Fermez la bouche	Close your mouth
Rincez	Rinse
Sentez-vous encore la douleur?	Does it hurt still?

14.1 Asking for help

14

In trouble

Help!	Au secours! *oa suhkoor!*
Fire!	Au feu! *oa fuh!*
Police!	Police! *pohlees!*
Quick!	Vite! *veet!*
Danger!	Danger! *dohnjhay*
Watch out!	Attention! *ahtohnsyawn!*
Stop!	Stop! *stop!*
Be careful!	Prudence! *prewdohns!*
Don't!	Arrêtez! *ahrehtay!*
Let go!	Lâchez! *lahshay!*
Stop that thief!	Au voleur! *oa voluhr!*
Could you help me, please?	Voulez-vous m'aider? *voolay voo mayday?*
Where's the police station/emergency exit/fire escape?	Où est le poste de police/la sortie de secours/l'escalier de secours? *oo eh luh post duh polees/lah sortee duh suhkoor/lehskahlyay duh suhkoor?*
Where's the nearest fire extinguisher?	Où y a-t-il un extincteur? *oo ee yah teel uhn nehxtahnktuhr?*
Call the fire brigade!	Prévenez les sapeurs-pompiers! *prayvuhnay lay sahpuhr pawnpyay!*
Call the police!	Appelez la police! *ahpuhlay lah polees!*
Call an ambulance!	Appelez une ambulance! *ahpuhlay ewn ohnbewlohns!*
Where's the nearest phone?	Où est le téléphone le plus proche? *oo eh luh taylayfon luh plew prosh?*
Could I use your phone?	Puis-je utiliser votre téléphone? *pwee jhuh ewteeleezay votr taylayfon?*
What's the emergency number?	Quel est le numéro d'urgence? *kehl eh luh newmayroa dewrjhons?*
What's the number for the police?	Quel est le numéro de téléphone de la police? *kehl eh luh newmayroa duh taylayfon duh lah polees?*

154

14.2 Loss

I've lost my purse/ _____ wallet	**J'ai perdu mon porte-monnaie/ portefeuille** *jhay pehrdew mawn port moneh/portfuhy*
I lost my...yesterday _____	**Hier j'ai oublié mon/ma...** *yehr jhay oobleeay mawn/mah...*
I left my...here _____	**J'ai laissé mon/ma...ici** *jhay layssay mawn/mah...eesee*
Did you find my...?	**Avez-vous trouvé mon/ma...?** *ahvay voo troovay mawn/mah...?*
It was right here _____	**Il était là** *eel ayteh lah*
It's quite valuable _____	**C'est un objet de valeur** *seh tuhn nobjheh duh vahluhr*
Where's the lost _____ property office?	**Où est le bureau des objets trouvés?** *oo eh luh bewroa day zobjheh troovay?*

14.3 Accidents

There's been an _____ accident	**Il y a eu un accident** *eel ee yah ew uhn nahkseedohn*
Someone's fallen into _____ the water	**Quelqu'un est tombé dans l'eau** *kehlkuhn eh tawnbay dohn loa*
There's a fire _____	**Il y a un incendie.** *eel ee yah uhn nahnsohndee*
Is anyone hurt? _____	**Y a-t-il quelqu'un de blessé?** *ee yah teel kehlkuhn duh blehssay?*
Some people have _____ been/no one's been injured	**Il (n)y a des(pas de) blessés** *eel (n)ee yah day(pah duh) blehssay*
There's someone in _____ the car/train still	**Il y a encore quelqu'un dans la voiture/le train** *eel ee ah ohnkor kehlkuhn dohn lah vwahtewr/luh trahn*

It's not too bad. Don't __ worry	**Ce n'est pas si grave. Ne vous inquiétez pas**
	suh neh pah see grahv. nuh voo zahnkyaytay pah
Leave everything the __ way it is, please	**Ne touchez à rien s'il vous plaît**
	nuh tooshay ah ryahn seel voo pleh
I want to talk to the ____ police first	**Je veux d'abord parler à la police**
	jhuh vuh dahbor pahrlay ah lah polees
I want to take a_____ photo first	**Je veux d'abord prendre une photo**
	jhuh vuh dahbor prohndr ewn foatoa
Here's my name _____ and address	**Voici mon nom et mon adresse**
	vwahsee mawn nawn ay mawn nahdrehs
Could I have your_____ name and address?	**Puis-je connaître votre nom et votre adresse?**
	pwee jhuh konehtr votr nawn ay votr ahdrehs?
Could I see some _____ dentification/your insurance papers?	**Puis-je voir vos papiers d'identité/papiers d'assurance?**
	pwee jhuh vwahr voa pahpyay deedohnteetay/pahpyay dahsewrohns?
Will you act as a_____ witness?	**Voulez-vous être témoin?**
	voolay voo zehtr taymwahn?
I need the details for ___ the insurance	**Je dois avoir les données pour l'assurance.**
	jhuh dwah zahvwahr lay donay poor lahsewrohns
Are you insured? _____	**Etes-vous assuré?** *eht voo zahsewray?*
Third party or _____ comprehensive?	**Responsabilité civile ou tous risques?**
	rehspawnsahbeeleetay seeveel oo too reesk?
Could you sign here, ___ please?	**Voulez-vous signer ici?**
	voolay voo seenyay eesee?

14.4 Theft

I've been robbed	On m'a volé.
	awn mah volay
My...has been stolen	Mon/ma...a été volé(e).
	mawn/mah...ah aytay volay
My car's been broken into	On a cambriolé ma voiture.
	awn nah kohnbreeolay mah vwahtewr

14.5 Missing person

I've lost my child/ grandmother	J'ai perdu mon enfant/ma grand-mère
	jhay pehrdew mawn nohnfohn/mah grohnmehr
Could you help me find him/her?	Voulez-vous m'aider à le/la chercher?
	voolay voo mayday ah luh/lah shehrshay?
Have you seen a small child?	Avez-vous vu un petit enfant?
	ahvay voo vew uhn puhtee tohnfohn?
He's/she's...years old	Il/elle a...ans.
	eel/ehl ah...ohn
He's/she's got short/long/blond/red/ brown/black/grey/ curly/ straight/frizzy hair	Il/elle a les cheveux courts/longs/blonds/ roux/bruns/noirs/gris/bouclés/raides/ frisés
	eel/ehl ah lay shuhvuh koor/lawn/blawn/roo/bruhn/nwahr/gree rehd/freezay
with a ponytail	avec une queue de cheval
	ahvehk ewn kuh duh shuhvahl
with plaits	avec des nattes
	ahvehk day naht
in a bun	avec un chignon
	ahvehk uhn sheenyawn
He's/she's got blue/brown/green eyes	Il/elle a les yeux bleus/bruns/verts
	eel/ehl ah lay zyuh bluh/bruhn/vehr

He's wearing _____ swimming trunks/ mountaineering boots	**Il porte un maillot de bain/des chaussures de montagne.** *eel port uhn mahyoa duh bahn/day shoasewr duh mawntahnyuh*
with/without glasses/ a bag	**avec/sans lunettes/un sac** *ahvehk/sohn lewneht/uhn sahk*
tall/short _____	**grand(e)/petit(e)** *grohn(d)/puhtee(t)*
This is a photo of _____ him/her	**Voici une photo de lui/d'elle.** *vwahsee ewn foatoa duh lwee/dehl*
He/she must be lost	**Il/elle s'est certainement égaré(e).** *eel/ehl seh sehrtehnmohn aygahray*

14.6 The police

An arrest

Vos papiers de voiture s'il vous plaît.	Your registration papers, please
Vous rouliez trop vite	You were speeding
Vous êtes en stationnement interdit	You're not allowed to park here
Vous n'avez pas mis d'argent dans le parcmètre	You haven't put money in the meter
Vos phares ne marchent pas	Your lights aren't working
Vous avez une contravention de...francs	That's a...franc fine
Vous voulez payer immédiatement?	Do you want to pay on the spot?
Vous devez payer immédiatement	You'll have to pay on the spot

| I don't speak French ___ | **Je ne parle pas français.** *jhuh nuh pahrl pah frohnseh* |

I didn't see the sign ____	Je n'ai pas vu ce panneau.
	jhuh nay pah vew suh pahnoa
I don't understand ____ what it says	Je ne comprends pas ce qu'il y est écrit.
	jhuh nuh kawnprohn pah suh keel ee yeh taykree
I was only doing... ____ kilometres an hour	Je ne roulais qu'à...kilomètres à l'heure.
	jhuh nuh rooleh kah...keeloamehtr ah luhr
I'll have my car ____ checked	Je vais faire réviser ma voiture.
	jhuh veh fehr rayveezay mah vwahtewr
I was blinded by ____ oncoming lights	J'ai été aveuglé(e) par une voiture en sens inverse.
	jhay aytay ahvuhglay pahr ewn vwahtewr ohn sohns ahnvehrs

At the police station

Où est-ce arrivé?	Where did it happen?
Qu'avez-vous perdu?	What's missing?
Qu'a-t-on volé?	What's been taken?
Puis-je voir vos papiers d'identité?	Do you have some identification?
A quelle heure est-ce arrivé?	What time did it happen?
Qui est en cause?	Who are the others?
Y a-t-il des témoins?	Are there any witnesses?
Voulez-vous remplir ceci?	Fill this out, please
Signez ici s'il vous plaît	Sign here, please
Voulez-vous un interprète?	Do you want an interpreter?

| I want to report a ____ collision/missing person/rape | Je viens faire la déclaration d'une collision/d'une disparition/d'un viol |
| | *jhuh vyahn fehr lah dayklahrasyawn dewn koleezyawn/dewn deespahreesyawn/duhn vyol* |

159

English	French
Could you make out a report, please?	Voulez-vous faire un rapport? *voolay voo fehr uhn rahpor?*
Could I have a copy for the insurance?	Puis-je avoir une copie pour l'assurance? *pwee jhahvwahr ewn kopee poor lahsewrohns?*
I've lost everything	J'ai tout perdu *jhay too pehrdew*
I'd like an interpreter	J'aimerais un interprète *jhehmuhreh zuhn nahntehrpreht*
I'm innocent	Je suis innocent(e) *jhuh swee zeenosohn(t)*
I don't know anything about it	Je ne sais rien *jhuh nuh seh ryahn*
I want to speak to someone from the British consulate	Je veux parler à quelqu'un du consulat britannique *jhuh vuh pahrlay ah kehlkuhn dew kawnsewlah breetahneek*
I need to see someone from the British embassy	Je dois parler à quelqu'un de l'ambassade britannique *jhuh dwah pahrlay ah kehlkuhn duh lohnbahsahd breetahneek*
I want a lawyer who speaks English	Je veux un avocat qui parle anglais *jhuh vuh uhn nahvokah kee pahrl ohngleh*

Word list English – French

● **This word list** is meant to supplement the previous chapters.
Nouns are always accompanied by the French definite article in order
to indicate whether it is a masculine (le) or feminine (la) word. In the
case of an abbreviated article (l'), the gender is indicated by (m.) or
(f.). In a number of cases, words not contained in this list can be
found elsewhere in this book, namely in the lists of the parts of the
car, the bicycle and the tent. Many food terms can be found in the
French-English list in 4.7.

A

about	environ	*ohnveerawn*
above	au-dessus	*oadsew*
abroad	l'étranger (m.)	*laytrohnjhay*
accident	l'accident (m.)	*lahkseedohn*
adder	la vipère	*lah veepehr*
addition	l'addition (f.)	*lahdeesyawn*
address	l'adresse (f.)	*lahdrehs*
admission	l'entrée (f.)	*lohntray*
admission price	le prix d'entrée	*luh pree dohntray*
advice	le conseil	*luh kawnsehy*
after	après	*ahpreh*
afternoon	l'après-midi (m., f.)	*lahpreh meedee*
aftershave	la lotion après -rasage	*lah loasyawn ahpreh rahzahjh*
again	à nouveau	*ah noovoa*
against	contre	*kawntr*
age	l'âge (m.)	*lahjh*
Aids	le sida	*luh seedah*
air conditioning	l'air conditionné (m.)	*lehr kawndeesyonay*
air mattress	le matelas pneumatique	*luh mahtlah pnuhmahteek*
air sickness bag	le petit sac à vomissements	*luh puhtee sahk ah vomeesmohn*
aircraft	l'avion (m.)	*lahvyawn*

airport	l'aéroport (m.)	*lahayroapor*
alarm	l'alarme (f.)	*lahlahrm*
alarm clock	le réveil	*luh rayvehy*
alcohol	l'alcool (m.)	*lahlkol*
A-level equivalent	le bac	*luh bahk*
a little	un peu	*uhn puh*
allergic	allergique	*ahlehrjheek*
alone	seul	*suhl*
always	toujours	*toojhoor*
ambulance	l'ambulance (f.)	*lohnbewlohns*
amount	le montant	*luh mawntohn*
amusement park	le parc d'attractions	*luh pahrk dahtrahksyawn*
anaesthetize	anesthésier	*ahnehstayzay*
anchovy	l'anchois (m.)	*lohnshwah*
and	et	*ay*
angry	en colère	*ohn kolehr*
animal	l'animal (m.)	*lahneemahl*
answer	la réponse	*lah raypawns*
ant	la fourmi	*lah foormee*
antibiotics	l'antibiotique (m.)	*lohnteebyoteek*
antifreeze	l'antigel (m.)	*lohnteejhehl*
antique	ancien	*ohnsyahn*
antiques	antiquités (f.)	*ohnteekeetay*
anus	l'anus (m.)	*lahnews*
apartment	l'appartement (m.)	*lahpahrtuhmohn*
aperitif	l'apéritif (m.)	*lahpayreeteef*
apologies	les excuses	*lay zehxkewz*
apple	la pomme	*lah pom*
apple juice	le jus de pommes	*luh jhew duh pom*
apple pie	la tarte aux pommes	*lah tahrt oa pom*
apple sauce	la compote de pommes	*lah kawnpot duh pom*
appointment	le rendez-vous	*luh rohndayvoo*
apricot	l'abricot (m.)	*lahbreekoa*
April	avril	*ahvreel*
archbishop	l'archevêque (m.)	*lahrshuhvehk*
architecture	l'architecture (f.)	*lahrsheetehktewr*
area	les environs	*lay zohnveerawn*

arm	le bras	*luh brah*
arrive	arriver	*ahreevay*
arrow	la flèche	*lah flehsh*
art	l'art (m.)	*lahr*
artery	l'artère (f.)	*lahrtehr*
artichoke	l'artichaut (m.)	*lahrteeshoa*
article	l'article (m.)	*lahrteekl*
artificial respiration	la respiration artificielle	*lah rehspeerahsyawn ahrteefeesyehl*
arts and crafts	l'artisanat d'art	*lahrteezahnah dahr*
ashtray	le cendrier	*luh sohndreeay*
ask	demander	*duhmohnday*
ask	prier	*preeay*
asparagus	les asperges	*lay zahspehrjh*
aspirin	l'aspirine (f.)	*lahspeereen*
assault	l'agression (f.)	*lahgrehsyawn*
at home	à la maison	*ah lah mehzawn*
at night	la nuit	*lah nwee*
at the back	à l'arrière	*ah lahryehr*
at the front	à l'avant	*ah lahvohn*
at the latest	au plus tard	*oa plew tahr*
aubergine	l'aubergine (f.)	*loabehrjheen*
August	août	*oot*
automatic	automatique	*loatoamahteek*
automatically	automatiquement	*oatoamahteekmohn*
autumn	l'automne (m.)	*loatonn*
avalanche	l'avalanche (f.)	*lahvahlohnsh*
awake	réveillé	*rayvay-yay*
awning	le parasol	*luh pahrahsol*

B

baby	le bébé	*luh baybay*
baby food	la nourriture pour bébé	*lah nooreetewr poor baybay*
babysitter	le/la baby-sitter	*luh/lah behbee seetehr*
back	le dos	*luh doa*
backpack	le sac à dos	*luh sahk ah doa*

bacon	le lard	*luh lahr*
bad	mauvais	*moaveh*
bag	le sac	*luh sahk*
baker (cakes)	le pâtissier	*luh pahteesyay*
baker	le boulanger	*luh boolohnjhay*
balcony (theatre)	le balcon	*luh bahlkawn*
balcony (to building)	le balcon	*luh bahlkawn*
ball	la balle	*lah bahl*
ballet	le ballet; la danse	*luh bahleh; la dohns*
ballpoint pen	le stylo à bille	*luh steeloa ah beey*
banana	la banane	*lah bahnahn*
bandage	le pansement	*luh pohnsmohn*
bank (river)	la rive	*lah reev*
bank	la banque	*lah bohnk*
bank card	la carte bancaire	*lah kahrt bohnkehr*
bar (café)	le bar	*luh bahr*
bar (drinks' cabinet)	le bar	*luh bahr*
barbecue	le barbecue	*luh bahrbuhkew*
bath	le bain	*luh bahn*
bath attendant	le maître nageur	*luh mehtr nahjhuhr*
bath foam	la mousse de bain	*lah moos duh bahn*
bath towel	la serviette de bain	*lah sehrvyeht duh bahn*
bathing cap	le bonnet de bain	*luh boneh duh bahn*
bathing cubicle	la cabine de bain	*lah kahbeen duh bahn*
bathing suit	le maillot de bain	*luh mahyoa duh bahn*
bathroom	la salle de bain	*lah sahl duh bahn*
battery (car)	l'accumulateur (m.)	*lahkewmewlahtuhr*
battery	la pile	*lah peel*
beach	la plage	*lah plahjh*
beans	les haricots	*lay ahreekoa*
beautiful	beau/belle	*boa/behl*
beautiful	magnifique	*mahnyeefeek*
beauty parlour	le salon de beauté	*luh sahlawn duh boatay*
bed	le lit	*luh lee*
bee	l'abeille (f.)	*lahbehy*
beef	la viande de boeuf	*lah vyohnd duh buhf*
beer	la bière	*lah byehr*

beetroot	la betterave	*lah behtrahv*
begin	commencer	*komohnsay*
beginner	le débutant	*luh daybewtohn*
behind	derrière	*dehryehr*
Belgian (f)	la belge	*lah behljh*
Belgian (m)	le belge	*luh behljh*
Belgium	la Belgique	*lah behljheek*
belt	la ceinture	*lah sahntewr*
berth	la couchette	*lah koosheht*
better	mieux	*myuh*
bicarbonate of soda	le bicarbonate de soude	*luh beekahrbonaht duh sood*
bicycle	la bicyclette/le vélo	*lah beeseekleht/luh vayloa*
bicycle pump	la pompe à bicyclette	*lah pawnp ah beeseekleht*
bicycle repairman	le réparateur de vélos	*luh raypahrahtuhr duh vayloa*
bikini	le bikini	*luh beekeenee*
bill	l'addition	*lahdeesyawn*
birthday	l'anniversaire (m.)	*lahneevehrsehr*
biscuit	le biscuit	*luh beeskwee*
bite	mordre	*mordr*
bitter	amer	*ahmehr*
black	noir	*nwahr*
bland	fade	*fahd*
blanket	la couverture	*lah koovehrtewr*
bleach	blondir	*blawndeer*
blister	la cloque	*lah klok*
blond	blond	*blawn*
blood	le sang	*luh sohn*
blood pressure	la tension	*lah tohnsyawn*
blouse	le chemisier	*luh shuhmeezyay*
blow dry	sécher	*sayshay*
blue	bleu	*bluh*
blunt	épointé/émoussé	*aypwahntay/aymoosay*
boat	le bateau	*luh bahtoa*
body	le corps	*luh kor*
body milk	le lait corporel	*luh leh korporehl*

boil	bouillir	*boo-yeer*
boiled	cuit	*kwee*
boiled ham	jambon cuit	*jhohnbawn kwee*
bone	l'os (m.)	*los*
bonnet	le capot	*luh kahpoa*
book (verb)	réserver	*raysehrvay*
book	le livre	*luh leevr*
booked	réservé	*rayzehrvay*
booking office	le bureau de	*luh bewroa duh*
	réservation	*rayzehrvahsyawn*
bookshop	la librairie	*lah leebrehree*
border	la frontière	*lah frawntyehr*
bored (to be)	s'ennuyer	*sonweeyay*
boring	ennuyeux	*onweeyuh*
born	né	*nay*
botanical gardens	le jardin botanique	*luh jhahrdahn botahneek*
both	tous/toutes les deux	*too/toot lay duh*
bottle-warmer	le chauffe-biberon	*luh shoaf beebrawn*
bottle (baby's)	le biberon	*luh beebrawn*
bottle	la bouteille	*lah bootehy*
box	la boîte	*lah bwaht*
box (theatre)	la loge	*lah lojh*
boy	le garçon	*luh gahrsawn*
bra	le soutien-gorge	*luh sootyahn gorjh*
bracelet	le bracelet	*luh brahsleh*
braised	braisé	*brehzay*
brake	le frein	*luh frahn*
brake fluid	le liquide de freins	*luh leekeed duh frahn*
brake oil	l'huile à frein (f.)	*lweel ah frahn*
bread	le pain	*luh pahn*
break	casser	*kahssay*
breakfast	le petit déjeuner	*luh puhtee dayjhuhnay*
breast	la poitrine	*lah pwahtreen*
bridge	le pont	*luh pawn*
briefs	la culotte	*lah kewlot*
brochure	la brochure	*lah broshewr*
broken	cassé	*kahssay*

broth	le consommé	*luh kawnsomay*
brother	le frère	*luh frehr*
brown	brun	*bruhn*
brush	la brosse	*lah bros*
Brussels sprouts	les choux de Bruxelles	*lay shoo duh brewxehl*
bucket	le seau	*luh soa*
bugs	les insectes nuisibles	*lay zahnsehkt nweezeebl*
building	le bâtiment	*luh bahteemohn*
buoy	la bouée	*lah booway*
burglary	le cambriolage	*luh kohnbryolajh*
burn (verb)	brûler	*brewlay*
burn	la brûlure	*lah brewlewr*
burnt	brûlé	*brewlay*
bus	l'autobus (m.)	*loatoabews*
bus station	la station d'autobus	*lah stahsyawn doatoabews*
bus stop	l'arrêt d'autobus (m.)	*lahreh doatoabews*
business class	la classe affaire (f.)	*lah klahs ahfehr*
business trip	le voyage d'affaires	*luh vwahyahjh dahfehr*
busy	animé	*ahneemay*
butane gas	le gaz butane	*luh gahz bewtahnn*
butcher	le boucher	*luh booshay*
butter	le beurre	*luh buhr*
button	le bouton	*luh bootawn*
buy	acheter	*ahshtay*
by airmail	la poste aérienne/ par avion	*lah post ahayryehn/ pahr ahvyawn*

C

cabbage	le chou	*luh shoo*
cabin	la cabine	*lah kahbeen*
cake	le gâteau	*luh gahtoa*
call	appeler	*ahpuhlay*
called (to be)	s'appeler	*sahpuhlay*
camera	l'appareil-photo (m.)	*lahpahrehy foatoa*

camp	faire du camping	*fehr dew kohnpeeng*
camp shop	le magasin du camping	*luh mahgahzahn dew kohnpeeng*
camp site	le camping	*luh kohnpeeng*
camper	le camping-car	*luh kohnpeeng kahr*
campfire	le feu de camp	*luh fuh duh kohn*
camping guide	le guide de camping	*luh gueed duh kohnpeeng*
camping permit	le permis de camping	*luh pehrmee duh kohnpeeng*
canal boat	la péniche	*lah payneesh*
cancel	annuler	*ahnewlay*
candle	la bougie	*lah boojhee*
canoe (verb)	faire du canoë	*fehr dew kahnoaeh*
canoe	le canoë	*luh kahnoaeh*
car (train)	le wagon	*luh vahgawn*
car	la voiture	*lah vwahtewr*
car deck	le pont à voitures	*luh pawn ah vwahtewr*
car documents	les papiers de voiture	*lay pahpyay duh vwahtewr*
car trouble	la panne	*lah pahnn*
carafe	la carafe	*lah kahrahf*
caravan	la caravane	*lah kahrahvahnn*
cardigan	le cardigan/le gilet	*luh kahrdeegahn/luh jheeleh*
careful	prudent	*prewdohn*
carrot	la carotte	*lah kahrot*
cartridge	la cartouche	*lah kahrtoosh*
cartridge	la cassette	*lah kahseht*
cascade	la cascade	*lah kahskahd*
cash desk	la caisse	*lah kehss*
casino	le casino	*luh kahzeenoa*
cassette	la cassette	*lah kahseht*
castle	le château	*luh shahtoa*
cat	le chat	*luh shah*
catalogue	le catalogue	*luh kahtahlog*
cathedral	la cathédrale	*lah kahtaydrahl*
cauliflower	le chou-fleur	*luh shoo fluhr*
cave	la grotte	*lah grot*

CD	le compact disc	*luh kawnpahkt deesk*
celebrate	célébrer	*saylaybray*
cellotape	le scotch	*luh skoch*
cemetery	le cimetière	*luh seemtyehr*
centimetre	le centimètre	*luh sohnteemehtr*
central heating	le chauffage central	*luh shoafahjh sohntrahl*
centre (in the)	au milieu	*oa meelyuh*
centre	le centre	*luh sohntr*
cereal	la céréale	*lah sayrayahl*
chair	la chaise	*lah shehz*
chambermaid	la femme de chambre	*lah fahm duh shohnbr*
chamois	la peau de chamois	*lah poa duh shahmwah*
champagne	le champagne	*luh shohnpany*
change (verb)	modifier	*modeefyay*
	changer	*shohnjhay*
change	la monnaie	*lah moneh*
change the baby's nappy	changer la couche du bébé	*shohnjhay lah koosh dew baybay*
change the oil	changer l'huile	*shohnjhay lweel*
chapel	la chapelle	*lah shahpehl*
charcoal tablets	les pastilles de charbon	*lay pahsteey duh shahrbawn*
charter flight	le vol charter	*luh vol shahrtehr*
chat up	draguer	*drahgay*
check (verb)	contrôler	*kawntroalay*
check in	enregistrer	*ohnruhjheestray*
cheers	à votre santé	*ah votr sohntay*
cheese	le fromage	*luh fromahjh*
chef	le chef	*luh shehf*
chemist	la pharmacie	*lah fahrmahsee*
cheque	le chèque	*luh shehk*
cherries	les cerises	*lay suhreez*
chess (play)	jouer aux échecs	*jhooay oa zayshehk*
chewing gum	le chewing-gum	*luh shweenguhm*
chicken	le poulet	*luh pooleh*
chicory	les endives	*lay zohndeev*
child	l'enfant (m./f.)	*lohnfohn*

child seat	le siège-enfant	*luh seeyehjh ohnfohn*
chilled	rafraîchi	*rahfrehshee*
chin	le menton	*luh montawn*
chips	les pommes-frites	*lay pom freet*
chocolate	le chocolat	*luh shoakoalah*
choose	choisir	*shwahzeer*
chop	la côtelette	*lah koatuhleht*
christian name	le prénom	*luh praynawn*
church	l'église (f.)	*laygleez*
church service	le service religieux	*luh sehrvees ruhleejhyuh*
cigar	le cigare	*luh seegahr*
cigar shop	le tabac	*luh tahbah*
cigarette	la cigarette	*lah seegahreht*
cigarette paper	le papier	*luh pahpyay ah*
	à cigarettes	*seegahreht*
cine camera	la caméra	*lah kahmayrah*
circle	le cercle	*luh sehrkl*
circus	le cirque	*luh seerk*
city	la ville	*lah veel*
map	le plan	*luh plohn*
classical concert	le concert classique	*luh kawnsehr klahsseek*
clean (verb)	nettoyer	*nehtwahyay*
clean	propre	*propr*
clear	clair	*klehr*
clearance	les soldes	*lay sold*
closed	fermé	*fehrmay*
closed off	bloqué	*blokay*
clothes	les habits	*lay zahbee*
clothes hanger	le cintre	*luh sahntr*
clothes peg	la pince à linge	*lah pahns ah lahnjh*
clothing	vêtements	*vehtmohn*
coach	l'autobus (m.)	*loatoabews*
coat	le manteau	*luh mohntoa*
cockroach	le cafard	*luh kahfahr*
cocoa	le cacao	*luh kahkahoa*
cod	le cabillaud	*luh kahbeeyoa*
coffee	le café	*luh kahfay*

coffee filter	le filtre de cafetière	*luh feeltr duh kahftyehr*
cognac	le cognac	*luh konyahk*
cold	froid	*frwah*
cold	le rhume	*luh rewm*
cold cuts	la charcuterie	*lah shahrkewtree*
collarbone	la clavicule	*lah klahveekewl*
colleague	le collègue	*luh kolehg*
collision	la collision	*lah koleezyawn*
cologne	l'eau de toilette (f.)	*loa duh twahleht*
colour	la couleur	*lah kooluhr*
colour pencils	les crayons de couleur	*lay krayawn duh kooluhr*
colour TV	la télévision	*lah taylayveezyawn*
	en couleurs	*ohn kooluhr*
colouring book	l'album de coloriage (m.)	*lahlbuhm duh koloryajh*
comb	le peigne	*luh pehnyuh*
come	venir	*vuhneer*
come back	revenir	*ruhvuhneer*
compartment	le compartiment	*luh kawnpahrteemohn*
complaint	la plainte	*lah plahnt*
complaints book	le cahier de	*luh kahyay duh*
	réclamations	*rayklahmahsyawn*
completely	entièrement	*ohntyehrmohn*
compliment	le compliment	*luh kawnpleemohn*
compulsory	obligatoire	*obleegahtwahr*
concert	le concert	*luh kawnsehr*
concert hall	la salle de concert	*lah sahl duh kawnsehr*
concussion	la commotion	*lah koamoasyawn*
	cérébrale	*sayraybrahl*
condensed milk	le lait condensé	*luh leh kawndohnsay*
condom	le préservatif	*luh prayzehrvahteef*
congratulate	féliciter	*fayleeseetay*
connection	la liaison	*lah lyehzawn*
constipation	la constipation	*lah kawnsteepahsyawn*
consulate	le consulat	*luh kownsewlah*
consultation	la consultation	*lah kawnsewltahsyawn*
contact lens	la lentille de contact	*lah lohnteey duh*
		kawntahkt

contact lens solution	le liquide pour	*luh leekeed poor*
	lentille de contact	*lohnteey duh kawntahkt*
contagious	contagieux	*kawntahjhyuh*
contraceptive	le contraceptif	*luh kawntrahsehpteef*
contraceptive pill	la pilule	*lah peelewl*
	anticonceptionnelle	*ohnteekawnsehpsyonehl*
convent	le couvent	*luh koovohn*
cook (verb)	cuisiner	*kweezeenay*
cook	le cuisinier	*luh kweezeenyay*
copper	le cuivre	*luh kweevr*
copy	la copie	*lah kopee*
corkscrew	le tire-bouchon	*luh teerbooshawn*
cornflour	la maïzena	*lah maheezaynah*
corner	le coin	*luh kwahn*
correct	correct	*korehkt*
correspond	correspondre	*korehspawndr*
corridor	le couloir	*luh koolwahr*
costume	le costume	*luh kostewm*
cot	le lit d'enfant	*luh lee dohnfohn*
cotton	le coton	*luh koatawn*
cotton wool	le coton	*luh koatawn*
cough	la toux	*lah too*
cough mixture	le sirop pectoral	*luh seeroa pehktoaral*
counter	la réception	*lah raysehpsyawn*
country	le pays	*luh pehy*
country	la campagne	*lah kohnpahnyuh*
country code	l'indicatif du pays (m.)	*lahndeekahteef dew pehy*
courgette	la courgette	*lah koorjheht*
cousin (f)	la cousine	*lah koozeen*
cousin (m)	le cousin	*luh koozahn*
crab	le crabe	*luh krahb*
cream	la crème	*lah krehm*
credit card	la carte de crédit	*lah kahrt duh kraydee*
crisps	les chips	*lay sheeps*
croissant	le croissant	*luh krwahssohn*
cross-country run	la piste de ski de fond	*lah peest duh skee duh fawn*
cross-country skiing	faire du ski de fond	*fehr dew skee duh fawn*

cross-country skis	les skis de fond	*lay skee duh fawn*
cross the road	traverser	*trahvehrsay*
crossing	la traversée	*lah trahvehrsay*
crossing	le croisement	*luh krwahzmohn*
cry	pleurer	*pluhray*
cubic metre	le mètre cube	*luh mehtr kewb*
cucumber	le concombre	*luh kawnkawnbr*
cuddly toy	l'animal en peluche (m.)	*lahneemahl ohn plewsh*
cuff links	les boutons de manchette	*lay bootawn duh mohnsheht*
cup	la tasse	*lah tahs*
curly	frisé	*freezay*
current	la circulation	*lah seerkewlahsyawn*
cushion	le coussin	*luh koossahn*
customary	habituel	*ahbeetewehl*
customs	la douane	*lah dwahnn*
customs	le contrôle douanier	*luh kawntrol dwahnnyay*
cut (verb)	couper	*koopay*
cutlery	couverts	*koovehr*
cycling	faire de la bicyclette/du vélo	*fehr duh lah beeseekleht/dew vayloa*

D

dairy produce	les produits laitiers	*lay prodwee laytyay*
damaged	abîmé	*ahbeemay*
dance	danser	*dohnsay*
dandruff	les pellicules	*lay payleekewl*
danger	le danger	*luh dohnjhay*
dangerous	dangereux	*dohnjhuhruh*
dark	sombre	*sawnbr*
date	le rendez-vous	*luh rohndayvoo*
daughter	la fille	*lah feey*
day	le jour	*luh jhoor*
day after tomorrow	après-demain	*ahpreh duhmahn*
day before yesterday	avant-hier	*ahvohn tyehr*

death	la mort	lah mor
decaffeinated	le décaféiné	luh daykahfayeenay
December	décembre	daysohnbr
deck chair	la chaise longue	lah shehz lawng
declare(customs)	déclarer	dayklahray
deep	profond	profawn
deep sea diving	la plongée sous-marine	lah plawnjhay soo mahreen
deepfreeze	le congélateur	luh kawnjhaylahtuhr
degrees	les degrés	lay duhgray
delay	le retard	luh ruhtahr
delicious	délicieux	dayleesyuh
dentist	le dentiste	luh dohnteest
dentures	le dentier	luh dohntyay
deodorant	le déodorant	luh dayodorohn
department	le rayon	luh rayawn
department store	le grand magasin	luh grohn mahgahzahn
departure	le départ	luh daypahr
departure time	l'heure de départ (f.)	ler duh daypahr
depilatory cream	la crème épilatoire	lah krehm aypeelahtwahr
deposit	arrhes, acompte	ahr, ahkawnt
dessert	le dessert	luh dehssehr
destination	la destination	lah dehsteenahsyawn
develop	développer	dayvlopay
diabetes	le diabète	luh deeahbeht
diabetic	le diabétique	luh dyahbayteek
dial	composer	kawnpoazay
diamond	le diamant	luh deeahmohn
diarrhoea	la diarrhée	lah deeahray
dictionary	le dictionnaire	luh deeksyonehr
diesel	le diesel	luh dyayzehl
diesel oil	le gas-oil	luh gahzwahl
diet	le régime	luh rayjheem
difficulty	la difficulté	lah deefeekewltay
dining room	la salle à manger	lah sahl ah mohnjhay
dining/buffet car	le wagon-restaurant	luh vahgawn rehstoaron
dinner (to have)	dîner	deenay
dinner	le dîner	luh deenay

dinner jacket	le smoking	*luh smokeeng*
direction	la direction	*lah deerehksyawn*
directly	directement	*deerehktuhmohn*
dirty	sale	*sahl*
disabled	l'invalide (m./f.)	*lahnvahleed*
disco	la discothèque	*lah deeskotehk*
discount	la réduction	*lah raydewksyawn*
disgusting	dégoûtant	*daygootohn*
dish	le plat	*luh plah*
dish of the day	le plat du jour	*luh plah dew jhoor*
disinfectant	le désinfectant	*luh dayzahnfehktohn*
distance	la distance	*lah deestohns*
distilled water	l'eau distillée (f.)	*loa deesteelay*
disturb	déranger	*dayrohnjhay*
disturbance	troubles, tapage	*troobl, tapahjh*
dive	plonger	*plawnjhay*
diving	la plongée	*lah plawnjhay*
diving board	le plongeoir	*luh plawnjhwahr*
diving gear	l'équipement	*laykeepmohn*
	de plongeur (m.)	*duh plawnjhuhr*
DIY-shop	le magasin	*luh mahgahzahn*
	de bricolage	*duh breekolajh*
dizzy	pris de vertige	*pree duh vehrteejh*
do (verb)	faire	*fehr*
doctor	le médecin	*luh maydsahn*
dog	le chien	*luh shyahn*
doll	la poupée	*lah poopay*
domestic	l'intérieur (m.) du pays	*lahntayryuhr dew pehy*
door	la porte	*lah port*
down	en bas	*ohn bah*
draught	le courant d'air	*luh koorohn dehr*
dream	rêver	*rehvay*
dress	la robe	*lah rob*
dressing gown	le peignoir	*luh paynywahr*
drink (verb)	boire	*bwahr*
drink	le verre	*luh vehr*
drinking chocolate	le chocolat au lait	*luh shoakoalah oa leh*

drinking water	l'eau potable (f.)	*loa potabl*
drive	conduire	*kawndweer*
driver	le chauffeur	*luh shoafuhr*
driving licence	le permis de conduire	*luh pehrmee duh kawndweer*
drought	la sécheresse	*lah sayshrehs*
dry (verb)	sécher	*sayshay*
dry	sec	*sehk*
dry clean	nettoyer à sec	*nehtwahyay ah sehk*
dry cleaner's	la teinturerie	*lah tahntewruhree*
dry shampoo	le shampooing sec	*luh shohnpwahn sehk*
dummy	la tétine	*lah tayteen*
during	pendant	*pohndohn*
during the day	de jour	*duh jhoor*

E

each time	chaque fois	*shahk fwah*
ear	l'oreille (f.)	*lorehy*
ear, nose and throat specialist (ENT)	l'oto-rhino (m.)	*loatoa reenoa*
earache	le mal d'oreille	*luh mahl dorehy*
eardrops	les gouttes pour les oreilles	*lay goot poor lay zorehy*
early	tôt	*toa*
earrings	les boucles d'oreilles	*lay bookl dorehy*
earth	la terre	*lah tehr*
earthenware	la poterie	*lah potree*
east	l'est (m.)	*lehst*
easy	facile	*fahseel*
eat	manger	*mohnjhay*
eczema	l'eczéma (m.)	*lehgzaymah*
eel	l'anguille (f.)	*lohngeey*
egg	l'oeuf (m.)	*luhf*
elastic band	l'élastique (m.)	*laylahsteek*
electric	électrique	*aylehktreek*
electric current	le courant	*luh koorohn*

electricity	l'électricité (f.)	*laylehktreeseetay*
embassy	l'ambassade (f.)	*lohnbahsahd*
emergency brake	le frein de secours	*luh frahn duh suhkoor*
emergency exit	la sortie de secours	*lah sortee duh suhkoor*
emergency number	le numéro d'urgence (m.)	*luh newmayroa dewrzhohns*
emergency phone	le téléphone d'urgence (m.)	*luh taylayfon dewrjhohns*
emergency triangle	le triangle de signalisation	*luh treeohngl duh seenyahleezahsyawn*
emery board	la lime à ongles	*lah leem ah awngl*
empty	vide	*veed*
engaged	occupé	*okewpay*
England	Angleterre	*ohngluhtehr*
English	anglais	*ohngleh*
entertainment guide	le journal des spectacles	*luh jhoornal day spehktahkl*
envelope	l'enveloppe (f.)	*lohnvlop*
escort	l'hôtesse	*loatehs*
evening	le soir	*luh swahr*
evening wear	la tenue de soirée	*lah tuhnew duh swahray*
event	l'évènement (m.)	*layvehnmohn*
everything	tout	*too*
everywhere	partout	*pahrtoo*
examine	examiner	*ehgzahmeenay*
excavation	les fouilles	*lay fooeey*
excellent	excellent	*ehxaylohn*
exchange	échanger	*ayshohnjhay*
exchange office	le bureau de change	*luh bewroa duh shohnjh*
exchange rate	le cours du change	*luh koor dew shohnjh*
excursion	l'excursion (f.)	*lehxkewrsyawn*
exhibition	l'exposition (f.)	*lehxpoazeesyawn*
exit	la sortie	*lah sortee*
expenses	les frais	*lay freh*
expensive	cher	*shehr*
explain	expliquer	*ehxpleekay*
express	l'express (m.)	*lehxprehs*
external	extérieur	*ehxtayryuhr*

eye	l'oeil (m.)	*luhy*
eye drops	les gouttes pour les yeux	*lay goot poor lay zyuh*
eye shadow	le fard à paupières	*luh fahr ah poapyehr*
eye specialist	l'ophtalmologue (m.)	*loftahmolog*
eyeliner	l'eye-liner (m.)	*lahy leehnehr*

F

face	le visage	*luh veezajh*
factory	l'usine (f.)	*lewzeen*
fair	la foire	*lah fwahr*
fall	tomber	*tawnbay*
family	la famille	*lah fahmeey*
famous	célèbre	*saylehbr*
far away	éloigné	*aylwahnyay*
farm	la ferme	*lah fehrm*
farmer	le fermier	*luh fehrmyay*
fashion	la mode	*lah mod*
fast	rapidement	*rahpeedmohn*
father	le père	*luh pehr*
fault	la faute	*lah foat*
fax	faxer	*fahxay*
fear	la peur	*lah puhr*
February	février	*fayvryay*
feel	sentir	*sohnteer*
feel like	avoir envie (de)	*ahvwahr ohnvee (duh)*
fence	la clôture	*lah kloatewr*
fever	la fièvre	*lah feeyehvr*
fill (tooth)	plomber	*plawnbay*
fill out	remplir	*rohnpleer*
filling	le plombage	*luh plawnbahjh*
film	la pellicule	*lah payleekewl*
filter	le filtre	*luh feeltr*
filthy	crasseux	*krahssuh*
find	trouver	*troovay*
fine	la caution	*lah koasyawn*
fine (parking)	la contravention	*lah kawntrahvohnsyawn*

finger	le doigt	*luh dwah*
fire	le feu	*luh fuh*
fire brigade	les sapeurs pompiers	*lay sahpuhr pawnpyay*
fire escape	l'escalier de secours (m.)	*lehskahlyay duh suhkoor*
fire extinguisher	l'extincteur (m.)	*lehxtahntuhr*
first	le premier	*luh pruhmyay*
first aid	les premiers soins	*lay pruhmyay swahn*
first class	la première classe	*lah pruhmyehr klahs*
fish (verb)	pêcher	*payshay*
fish	le poisson	*luh pwahssawn*
fishing rod	la canne à pêche	*lah kahnn ah pehsh*
fitness centre	le centre de	*luh sohntr duh*
	mise en forme	*meez ohn form*
fitness training	l'entraînement de	*lohntrehnmohn duh*
	mise en forme (m.)	*meez ohn form*
fitting room	la cabine d'essayage	*lah kahbeen dehsayahjh*
fix	réparer	*raypahray*
flag	le drapeau	*luh drahpoa*
flash bulb	l'ampoule de flash (f.)	*lohnpool duh flahsh*
flash cube	le cube-flash	*luh kewb flahsh*
flash gun	le flash	*luh flahsh*
flat	l'appartement (m.)	*lahpahrtuhmohn*
flea market	le marché aux puces	*luh mahrshay oa pews*
flight	le vol	*luh vol*
flight number	le numéro de vol	*luh newmayroa duh vol*
flood	l'inondation (f.)	*leenawndahsyawn*
floor	l'étage (m.)	*laytahjh*
flour	la farine	*lah fahreen*
flu	la grippe	*lah greep*
fly-over	l'autopont (m.)	*loatoapawn*
fly (insect)	la mouche	*lah moosh*
fly (verb)	voler	*volay*
fog	le brouillard	*luh brooy-yahr*
foggy (to be)	faire du brouillard	*fehr dew brooy-yahr*
folding caravan	la caravane pliante	*lah kahrahvahnn pleeohnt*
follow	suivre	*sweevr*
food	la nourriture	*lah nooreetewr*

food poisoning	l'intoxication alimentaire (f.)	*lahntoxeekahsyawn ahleemohntehr*
foodstuffs	les produits alimentaires	*lay prohdwee zahleemohntehr*
foot	le pied	*luh pyay*
for hire	à louer	*ah looay*
forbidden	interdit	*ahntehrdee*
forehead	le front	*luh frawn*
foreign	étranger	*aytrohnjhay*
forget	oublier	*oobleeay*
fork	la fourchette	*lah foorsheht*
form	le questionnaire	*luh kehstyonehr*
fort	le fort	*luh for*
fountain	la fontaine	*lah fawntehn*
four star petrol	le super	*luh sewpehr*
frame	la monture	*lah mawntewr*
franc	le franc	*luh frohn*
free	libre	*leebr*
free of charge	gratuit	*grahtwee*
free time	les loisirs	*lay lwahzeer*
freeze	geler	*jhuhlay*
French	français	*frohnseh*
French (language)	le français	*luh frohnseh*
French bread	la baguette	*lah bahgeht*
fresh	frais	*freh*
Friday	vendredi	*vohndruhdee*
fried	frit	*free*
fried egg	l'oeuf sur le plat (m.)	*luhf sewr luh plah*
friend	l'ami(e) (m./f.)	*lahmee*
friendly	amical	*ahmeekahl*
fringe	la frange	*lah frohnjh*
fruit	le fruit	*luh frwee*
fruit juice	le jus de fruits	*luh jhew duh frwee*
frying pan	la poêle à frire	*lah pwahl ah freer*
full	plein	*plahn*
fun	le plaisir	*luh playzeer*
funny	drôle	*droal*

G

gallery	la galerie	*lah gahlree*
game	le jeu	*luh jhuh*
garage	le garage	*luh gahrahjh*
garbage bag	le sac poubelle	*luh sahk poobehl*
garden	le jardin	*luh jhahrdahn*
gastroenteritis	la gastro-entérite	*gahstroa ohntayreet*
gauze	la compresse de gaze	*lah kawnprehs duh gahz*
gel	le gel	*luh jhehl*
German	allemand	*ahlmohn*
get married	(se) marier	*(suh) mahryay*
get off	descendre	*daysohndr*
gift	le cadeau	*luh kahdoa*
gilt	doré	*doray*
ginger	le gingembre	*luh jhahnjhohnbr*
girl	la fille	*lah feey*
girlfriend	l'amie	*lahmee*
giro card	la carte de chèque postal	*lah kahrt duh shehk postahl*
giro cheque	le chèque postal	*luh shehk postahl*
glacier	le glacier	*luh glahsyay*
glass (wine -)	le verre	*luh vehr*
glasses (sun -)	les lunettes	*lay lewneht*
glide	faire du vol à voile	*fehr dew vol ah vwahl*
glove	le gant	*luh gohn*
glue	la colle	*lah kol*
go	aller	*ahlay*
go back	reculer, retourner	*ruhkewlay, ruhtoornay*
go out	sortir	*sorteer*
goat's cheese	le fromage de chèvre	*luh fromajh duh shehvr*
gold	l'or (m.)	*lor*
golf course	le terrain de golf	*luh tehrahn duh golf*
good afternoon	bonjour	*bawnjhoor*
good evening	bonsoir	*bawnswahr*
good morning	bonjour	*bawnjhoor*
good night	bonne nuit	*bon nwee*

goodbye	au revoir	*oa ruhvwahr*
gram	le gramme	*luh grahm*
grandchild	le petit enfant	*luh puhtee tohnfohn*
grandfather	le grand-père	*luh grohn pehr*
grandmother	la grand-mère	*lah grohn mehr*
grape juice	le jus de raisin	*luh jhew duh rayzahn*
grapefruit	le pamplemousse	*luh pohnpluhmoos*
grapes	les raisins	*lay rayzahn*
grass	l'herbe (f.)	*lehrb*
grave	la tombe	*lah townb*
greasy	gras	*grah*
green	vert	*vehr*
green card	la carte verte	*lah kahrt vehrt*
greet	saluer	*sahleway*
grey	gris	*gree*
grill	griller	*greeyay*
grilled	grillé	*greeyay*
grocer	l'épicier (m)	*laypeesyay*
ground	le sol	*luh sol*
group	le groupe	*luh groop*
guest house	la pension	*lah pohnsyawn*
guide (book)	le guide	*luh gueed*
guide (person)	le/la guide	*luh/lah gueed*
guided tour	la visite guidée	*lah veezeet gueeday*
gynaecologist	le gynécologue	*luh jheenaykolog*

H

hair	les cheveux	*lay shuhvuh*
hairbrush	la brosse à cheveux	*lah bros ah shuhvuh*
hairdresser	le coiffeur	*luh kwahfuhr*
hairslides	les barrettes	*lay bahreht*
hairspray	la laque	*lah lahk*
half (adj.)	demi	*duhmee*
half	la moitié	*lah mwahtyay*
half full	à moitié plein	*ah mwahtyay plahn*
hammer	le marteau	*luh mahrtoa*

hand	la main	lah mahn
hand brake	le frein à main	luh frahn ah mahn
handbag	le sac à main	luh sahk ah mahn
handkerchief	le mouchoir	luh mooshwahr
handmade	fait-main	feh mahn
happy	heureux	uhruh
harbour	le port	luh por
hard	dur	dewr
hat	le chapeau	luh shahpoa
hay fever	le rhume des foins	luh rewm day fwahn
hazelnut	la noisette	lah nwahzeht
head	la tête	lah teht
headache	le mal de tête	luh mahl duh teht
headscarf	le foulard	luh foolahr
health	la santé	lah sohntay
health food shop	le magasin diététique	luh mahgahzahn dyaytayteek
hear	entendre	ohntohndr
hearing aid	la correction auditive	lah korehksyawn oadeeteev
heart	le coeur	luh kuhr
heater	le chauffage	luh shoafahjh
heavy	lourd	loor
heel	le talon	luh tahlawn
hello	bonjour, salut	bawnjhoor, sahlew
helmet	le casque	luh kahsk
help (verb)	aider	ayday
help	l'aide (f.)	lehd
herbal tea	l'infusion (f.)	lahnfewzyawn
here	ici	eesee
herring	le hareng	luh ahrohn
high	haut	oa
high tide	le flux	luh flew
highchair	la chaise d'enfant	lah shehz dohnfohn
hiking	la marche à pied	lah mahrsh ah pyay
hiking trip	la randonnée	lah rohndonay
hip	la hanche	lah ohnsh
hire	louer	looay

hitchhike	faire de l'auto-stop	_fehr duh loatoastop_
hobby	le passe-temps	_luh pahstohn_
hold-up	l'attaque (f.)	_lahtahk_
holiday house	la maison de vacances	_lah mehzawn duh vahkohns_
holidays	les vacances	_lay vahkohns_
homesickness	le mal du pays	_luh mahl dew pehy_
honest	honnête	_oneht_
honey	le miel	_luh myehl_
horizontal	horizontal	_oareezawntahl_
horrible	horrible	_oareebl_
horse	le cheval	_luh shuhvahl_
hospital	l'hôpital (m.)	_loapeetahl_
hospitality	l'hospitalité(f.)	_lospeetahleetay_
hot	chaud	_shoa_
hot-water bottle	la bouillotte	_lah booy-yot_
hot (spicy)	pimenté	_peemohntay_
hotel	l'hôtel (m.)	_loatehl_
hour	l'heure (f.)	_luhr_
house	la maison	_lah mehzawn_
household appliances	les appareils	_lay zahpahrehy_
houses of parliament	le parlement	_luh pahrluhmohn_
housewife	la femme au foyer	_lah fahm oa fwahyay_
how far?	c'est loin?	_seh lwahn?_
how long?	combien de temps?	_kawnbyahn duh tohn?_
how much?	combien?	_kawnbyahn?_
how?	comment?	_komohn?_
hungry (to be)	avoir faim	_ahvwahr fahn_
hurricane	l'ouragan (m.)	_loorahgohn_
hurry	la hâte	_lah aht_
husband	le mari	_luh mahree_
hut	la cabane	_lah kahbahnn_
hyperventilation	l'hyperventilation (f.)	_leepehrvohnteelahsyawn_

ice cream	la glace	*lah glahs*
ice cubes	les glaçons	*lay glahsawn*
ice skate	patiner	*pahteenay*
idea	l'idée (f.)	*leeday*
identification	la pièce d'identité	*lah pyehs deedohnteetay*
identify	identifier	*eedohnteefyay*
ignition key	la clef de contact	*lah klay duh kawntahkt*
ill	malade	*mahlahd*
illness	la maladie	*lah mahlahdee*
imagine	imaginer	*eemahjheenay*
immediately	immédiatement	*eemaydyahtmohn*
import duty	les droits de douane	*lay drwah duh dwahnn*
impossible	impossible	*ahnposeebl*
in	dans	*dohn*
in the evening	le soir	*luh swahr*
in the morning	le matin	*luh mahtahn*
included	compris	*kawnpree*
indicate	indiquer	*ahndeekay*
indicator	le clignotant	*luh kleenyotohn*
inexpensive	bon marché	*bawn mahrshay*
infection (viral/ bacterial)	l'infection (virale/ bactérielle) (f.)	*lahnfehksyawn (veerahl, bahktayryehl)*
inflammation	l'inflammation (f.)	*lahnflahmahsyawn*
information	l'information (f.)	*lahnformahsyawn*
information	le renseignement	*luh rohnsehnymohn*
information office	le bureau de renseignements	*luh bewroa duh rohnsehnymohn*
injection	la piqûre	*lah peekewr*
injured	blessé	*blehssay*
inner ear	l'oreille interne (f.)	*lorehy ahntehrn*
inner tube	la chambre à air	*lah shohnbr ah ehr*
innocent	innocent	*eenosohn*
insect	l'insecte (m.)	*lahnsehkt*
insect bite	la piqûre d'insecte	*lah peekewr dahnsehkt*

insect repellant	l'huile contre	*lweel kawntr*
	les moustiques	*lay moosteek*
inside	à l'intérieur	*ah lahntayryuhr*
instructions	le mode d'emploi	*luh mod dohnplwah*
insurance	l'assurance (f.)	*lahsewrohns*
intermission	la pause	*lah poaz*
international	international	*ahntehrnahsyonahl*
interpreter	l'interprète (m./f.)	*lahntehrpreht*
intersection	le carrefour	*luh kahrfoor*
introduce oneself	se présenter	*suh prayzohntay*
invite	inviter	*ahnveetay*
invoice	la facture	*lah fahktewr*
iodine	l'iode (m.)	*lyod*
Ireland	l'Irlande (f.)	*leerlohnd*
Irish	irlandais	*leerlohndeh*
iron (verb)	repasser	*ruhpahsay*
iron	le fer à repasser	*luh fehr ah ruhpahsay*
ironing board	la table à repasser	*lah tahbl ah ruhpahsay*
island	l'île (f.)	*leel*
it's a pleasure	je vous en prie	*jhuh voo zohn pree*
Italian	italien	*eetahlyahn*
itch	la démangeaison	*lah daymohnjhehzawn*

J

jack	le cric	*luh kreek*
jacket	la veste	*lah vehst*
jam	la confiture	*lah kawnfeetewr*
January	janvier	*jhohnvyay*
jaw	la mâchoire	*lah mahshwahr*
jellyfish	la méduse	*lah maydewz*
jeweller	le bijoutier	*luh beejhootyay*
jewellery	les bijoux	*lay beejhoo*
jog	faire du jogging	*fehr dew jogeeng*
joke	la blague	*lah blahg*
juice	le jus	*luh jhew*
July	juillet	*jhweeyeh*

jump leads	le câble de démarrage	*luh kahbl duh daymahrahjh*
jumper	le pull-over	*luh pewlovehr*
June	juin	*jhwahn*

K

key	la clef/clé	*lah klay*
kilo	le kilo	*luh keeloa*
kilometre	le kilomètre	*luh keeloamehtr*
king	le roi	*luh rwah*
kiss (verb)	embrasser	*ohnbrahssay*
kiss	le baiser	*luh bayzay*
kitchen	la cuisine	*lah kweezeen*
knee	le genou	*luh jhuhnoo*
knee socks	les mi-bas	*lay mee bah*
knife	le couteau	*luh kootoa*
knit	tricoter	*treekotay*
know	savoir	*sahvwahr*

L

lace	la dentelle	*lah dohntehl*
ladies' toilets	les toilettes pour dames	*lay twahleht poor dahm*
lake	le lac	*luh lahk*
lamp	la lampe	*lah lohnp*
land	atterrir	*ahtayreer*
lane	la voie	*lah vwah*
language	la langue	*lah lohng*
large	grand	*grohn*
last	dernier, passé	*dehrnyay, pahssay*
last night	la nuit passée	*lah nwee pahssay*
late	tard	*tahr*
later	tout à l'heure	*too tah luhr*
laugh	rire	*reer*
launderette	la laverie automatique	*lah lahvree oatoamahteek*
law	la loi	*lah lwah*
laxative	le laxatif	*luh lahxahteef*

leaky	crevé	*kruhvay*
leather	le cuir	*luh kweer*
leather goods	les articles	*lay zahrteekl*
	de maroquinerie	*duh mahrokeenree*
leave	partir	*pahrteer*
leek	le poireau	*luh pwahroa*
left	gauche	*goash*
left luggage	la consigne	*lah kawnseeny*
left, on the	à gauche	*ah goash*
leg	la jambe	*lah jhohnb*
lemon	le citron	*luh seetrawn*
lemonade	la limonade	*lah leemonahd*
lend	prêter (à)	*prehtay (ah)*
lens	la lentille	*lah lohnteey*
lentils	les lentilles	*lay lohnteey*
less	moins	*mwahn*
lesson	la leçon	*lah luhsawn*
letter	la lettre	*lah lehtr*
lettuce	la laitue	*lah laytew*
level crossing	le passage à niveau	*luh pahssahjh ah neevoa*
library	la bibliothèque	*lah beebleeotehk*
lie (down)	s'étendre	*saytohndr*
lie (verb)	mentir	*mohnteer*
hitch-hiking	l'auto-stop	*loatoastop*
lift (in building)	l'ascenseur (m.)	*lahsohnsuhr*
lift (chair)	le télésiège	*luh taylaysyehjh*
light (not dark)	clair	*klehr*
light (not heavy)	léger	*layjhay*
light	la lumière	*lah lewmyehr*
lighter	le briquet	*luh breekeh*
lighthouse	le phare	*luh fahr*
lightning	la foudre	*lah foodr*
like	aimer	*aymay*
line	la ligne	*lah leenyuh*
linen	le lin	*luh lahn*
lipstick	le rouge à lèvres	*luh roojh ah lehvr*
liquorice	le réglisse	*luh rayglees*

listen	écouter	*aykootay*
literature	la littérature	*lah leetayrahtewr*
litre	le litre	*luh leetr*
little	peu	*puh*
live	habiter	*ahbeetay*
live	vivre	*veevr*
live together	habiter ensemble	*ahbeetay ohnsohnbl*
lobster	le homard	*luh omahr*
locally	localement	*lokahlmohn*
lock	la serrure	*lah sehrewr*
long	long	*lawn*
look	regarder	*ruhgahrday*
look for	chercher	*shehrshay*
look up	rechercher	*ruhshehrshay*
lorry	le camion	*luh kahmyawn*
lose	perdre	*pehrdr*
loss	la perte	*lah pehrt*
lost	introuvable, perdu	*ahntroovahbl, pehrdew*
lost item	l'objet perdu (m.)	*lohbjeh pehrdew*
lost property office	les objets trouvés	*lay zobjheh troovay*
lotion	la lotion	*lah loasyawn*
loud	fort	*for*
love (to be in)	être amoureux	*ehtr ahmooruh*
love (verb)	aimer	*aymay*
love	l'amour (m.)	*lahmoor*
low	bas	*bah*
low tide	le reflux	*luh ruhflew*
luck	la chance	*lah shohns*
luggage	le bagage	*luh bahgahjh*
luggage locker	la consigne automatique	*lah kawnseenyuh oatoamahteek*
lunch	le déjeuner	*luh dayjhuhnay*
lunchroom	le café	*luh kahfay*
lungs	les poumons	*lay poomawn*

macaroni	les macaronis	*lay mahkahroanee*
madam	madame	*mahdahm*
magazine	la revue	*lah ruhvew*
mail	le courrier	*luh kooryay*
main post office	le bureau de poste central	*luh bewroa duh post sohntral*
main road	la grande route	*lah grohnd root*
make an appointment	prendre un rendez-vous	*prohndr uhn rohndayvoo*
make love	faire l'amour	*fehr lahmoor*
makeshift	provisoirement	*proveezwahrmohn*
man	l'homme (m.)	*lom*
manager	le directeur	*luh deerehktuhr*
mandarin	la mandarine	*lah mohndahreen*
manicure	la manucure	*lah mahnewkewr*
map	la carte géographique	*lah kahrt jhayoagrahfeek*
marble	le marbre	*luh mahrbruh*
March	mars	*mahrs*
margarine	la margarine	*lah mahrgahreen*
marina	le port de plaisance	*luh por duh playzohns*
market	le marché	*luh mahrshay*
marriage	le mariage	*luh mahryajh*
married	marié	*mahreeay*
mass	la messe	*lah mehs*
massage	le massage	*luh mahsahjh*
mat	mat	*maht*
match	le match	*luh mahch*
matches	les allumettes	*lay zahlewmeht*
May	mai	*meh*
maybe	peut-être	*puh tehtr*
mayonnaise	la mayonnaise	*lah mahyonehz*
mayor	le maire	*luh mehr*
meal	le repas	*luh ruhpah*
mean	signifier	*seenyeefyay*
meat	la viande	*lah vyohnd*

medical insurance	l'assurance maladie (f.)	*lahsewrohns mahlahdee*
medication	le médicament	*luh maydeekahmohn*
medicine	le médicament	*luh maydeekahmohn*
meet	rencontrer	*rohnkohntray*
melon	le melon	*luh muhlawn*
membership	l'adhésion (f.)	*lahdayzyawn*
menstruate	avoir ses règles	*ahvwahr say rehgl*
menstruation	les règles	*lay rehgl*
menu	la carte	*lah kahrt*
menu of the day	le menu du jour	*luh muhnew dew jhoor*
message	le message	*luh mehsahjh*
metal	le métal	*luh maytahl*
meter	le compteur	*luh kawntuhr*
metre	le mètre	*luh mehtr*
migraine	la migraine	*lah meegrehn*
mild (tobacco)	léger	*layjhay*
milk	le lait	*luh leh*
millimetre	le millimètre	*luh meeleemehtr*
milometer	le compteur kilométrique	*luh kawntuhr keeloamaytreek*
mince	la viande hachée	*lah vyohnd ahshay*
mineral water	l'eau minérale (f.)	*loa meenayral*
minute	la minute	*lah meenewt*
mirror	le miroir	*luh meerwahr*
miss	manquer	*mohnkay*
missing (to be)	manquer	*mohnkay*
mistake	l'erreur (f.)	*lehruhr*
misunderstanding	le malentendu	*luh mahlohntohndew*
mocha	le moka	*luh mokah*
modern art	l'art moderne (m.)	*lahr modehrn*
molar	la molaire	*lah molehr*
moment	le moment	*luh momohn*
Monday	lundi	*luhndee*
money	l'argent (m.)	*lahrjhohn*
month	le mois	*luh mwah*
moped	le cyclomoteur	*luh seekloamotuhr*
morning-after pill	la pilule du lendemain	*lah peelewl dew lohnduhmahn*

mosque	la mosquée	*lah moskay*
motel	le motel	*luh moatehl*
mother	la mère	*lah mehr*
moto-cross	le moto-cross	*luh moatoakros*
motorbike	la motocyclette	*lah moatoaseekleht*
motorboat	le bateau à moteur	*luh bahtoa ah motuhr*
motorway	l'autoroute (f.)	*loatoaroot*
mountain	la montagne	*lah mawntanyuh*
mountain hut	le refuge	*luh ruhfewjh*
mountaineering	l'alpinisme (m.)	*lahlpeeneesm*
mountaineering shoes	les chaussures de montagne	*lay shoasewr duh mawntanyuh*
mouse	la souris	*lah sooree*
mouth	la bouche	*lah boosh*
much/many	beaucoup	*boakoo*
multi-storey car park	le parking	*luh pahrkeeng*
muscle	le muscle	*luh mewskl*
muscle spasms	les crampes musculaires	*lay krohnp mewskewlehr*
museum	le musée	*luh mewzay*
mushrooms	les champignons	*lay shohnpeenyawn*
music	la musique	*lah mewzeek*
musical	la comédie musicale	*lah komaydee mewzeekahl*
mussels	les moules	*lay mool*
mustard	la moutarde	*lah mootahrd*

N

nail (on hand)	l'ongle (m.)	*lawngl*
nail	le clou	*luh kloo*
nail polish	le vernis à ongles	*luh vehrnee ah awngl*
nail polish remover	le dissolvant	*luh deesolvohn*
nail scissors	le coupe-ongles	*luh koop awngl*
naked	nu	*new*
nappy	la couche	*lah koosh*
nationality	la nationalité	*lah nahsyonahleetay*
natural	naturel	*nahtewrehl*
nature	la nature	*lah nahtewr*

naturism	le naturisme (m.)	*luh nahtewreesm*
nauseous	(avoir) mal au coeur	*(ahvwahr) mahl oa kuhr*
near	près	*preh*
nearby	tout près	*too preh*
necessary	nécessaire	*naysehsehr*
neck	le collier	*luh kolyay*
necklace	la chaîne	*lah shehn*
nectarine	la nectarine	*lah nehktahreen*
needle	l'aiguille (f.)	*laygweey*
negative	le négatif	*luh naygahteef*
neighbours	les voisins	*lay vwahzahn*
nephew	le neveu	*luh nuhvuh*
Netherlands	les Pays-Bas	*lay pehy bah*
never	jamais	*jhahmeh*
new	nouveau	*noovoa*
news	les informations	*lay zahnformahsyawn*
news stand	le kiosque	*luh kyosk*
newspaper	le journal	*luh jhoornahl*
next	le prochain	*luh proshahn*
next to	à côté de	*ah koatay duh*
nice (friendly)	gentil	*jhohntee*
nice	agréable, bon	*ahgrayahbl, bawn*
niece	la nièce	*lah nyehs*
night	la nuit	*lah nwee*
night duty	le service de nuit	*luh sehrvees duh nwee*
nightclub	la boîte de nuit/	*lah bwaht duh nwee/*
	le night-club	*luh naheet kluhb*
nightlife	la vie nocturne	*lah vee noktewrn*
nipple	la tétine	*lah tayteen*
no-one	personne	*pehrson*
no	non	*nawn*
no overtaking	l'interdiction	*lahntehrdeeksyawn*
	de dépasser (f.)	*duh daypahsay*
noise	le bruit	*luh brwee*
nonstop	continu	*kawnteenew*
normal	normal, ordinaire	*normahl, ordeenehr*
north	le nord	*luh nor*

nose	le nez	*luh nay*
nose bleed	le saignement de nez	*luh sehnyuhmohn dew nay*
nose drops	les gouttes pour le nez	*lay goot poor luh nay*
notepaper	le papier postal	*luh pahpyay postahl*
nothing	rien	*ryahn*
November	novembre	*novohnbr*
nowhere	nulle part	*newl pahr*
nudist beach	la plage de nudistes	*lah plahjh duh newdeest*
number	le numéro	*luh newmayroa*
number plate	la plaque d'immatriculation	*lah plahk deemahtree-kewlahsyawn*
nurse	l'infirmière (f.)	*lahnfeermyehr*
nutmeg	la noix de muscade	*lah nwah duh mewskahd*
nuts	les noix	*lay nwah*

O

October	octobre	*oktobr*
off licence	le marchand de vin	*luh mahrshohn duh vahn*
offer	offrir	*ofreer*
office	le bureau	*luh bewroa*
oil	l'huile (f.)	*lweel*
oil level	le niveau d'huile	*luh neevoa dweel*
ointment	le baume	*luh boam*
ointment for burns	la pommade contre les brûlures	*lah pomahd kawntr lay brewlewr*
okay	d'accord	*dahkor*
old	vieux	*vyuh*
old town	la vieille ville	*lah vyehy veel*
olive oil	l'huile d'olive	*lweel doleev*
olives	les olives	*lay zoleev*
omelette	l'omelette (f.)	*lomleht*
on	sur	*sewr*
on board	à bord	*ah bor*
on the way	en cours de route	*ohn koor duh root*
oncoming car	le véhicule en sens inverse	*luh vayeekewl ohn sohns ahnvehr*

one-way traffic	la circulation	*lah seerkewlahsyawn*
	à sens unique	*ah sohns ewneek*
one hundred grams	cent grammes	*sohn grahm*
onion	l'oignon (m.)	*lonyawn*
open (verb)	ouvrir	*oovreer*
open	ouvert	*oovehr*
opera	l'opéra (m.)	*loapayrah*
operate	opérer	*oapayray*
operator (telephone)	la téléphoniste	*lah taylayfoneest*
operetta	l'opérette (f.)	*loapayreht*
opposite	en face	*ohn fahs*
optician	l'opticien (m.)	*lopteesyahn*
or	ou	*oo*
orange	l'orange (f.)	*lorohnjh*
orange (adj.)	orange	*orohnjh*
orange juice	le jus d'orange	*luh jhew dorohnjh*
order (verb)	commander	*komohnday*
order	la commande	*lah kohmohnd*
other	l'autre	*loatr*
other side	l'autre côté	*loatr koatay*
outside	dehors	*duh-or*
overtake	doubler	*dooblay*
oysters	les huîtres	*lay zweetr*

P

package (post)	le paquet postal	*luh pahkeh postahl*
packed lunch	le casse-croûte	*luh kahs kroot*
page	la page	*lah pahjh*
pain	la douleur	*lah dooluhr*
painkiller	le calmant	*luh kahlmohn*
paint	la peinture	*lah pahntewr*
painting (art)	le tableau	*luh tahbloa*
palace	le palais	*luh pahleh*
pan	la casserole	*lah kahsrol*
pancake	la crêpe	*lah krehp*
pane	la vitre	*lah veetr*

pants	la culotte	*lah kewlot*
panty liner	le protège-slip	*luh protehjh sleep*
paper	le papier	*luh pahpyay*
paraffin oil	le pétrole	*luh paytrol*
parasol	le parasol	*luh pahrahsol*
parcel	le colis	*luh kolee*
pardon	pardon	*pahrdawn*
parents	les parents	*lay pahrohn*
park	le parc	*luh pahrk*
park (verb)	garer	*gahray*
parking space	la place de parking	*lah plahs duh pahrkeeng*
parsley	le persil	*luh pehrsee*
part	la pièce	*lah pyehs*
partition	la séparation	*lah saypahrahsyawn*
partner	le/la partenaire	*luh/lah pahrtuhnehr*
party	la fête	*lah feht*
passable	praticable	*prahteekahbl*
passenger	le passager	*luh pahsahjhay*
passport	le passeport	*luh pahspor*
passport photo	la photo d'identité	*lah foatoa deedohnteetay*
patient	le patient	*luh pahsyohn*
pavement	le trottoir	*luh trotwahr*
pay	payer	*payay*
peach	la pêche	*lah pehsh*
peanuts	les cacahuètes	*lay kahkahweht*
pear	la poire	*lah pwahr*
peas	les petits pois	*lay puhtee pwah*
pedal	la pédale	*lah paydahl*
pedestrian crossing	le passage clouté	*luh pahsahjh klootay*
pedicure	le/la pédicure	*luh/lah paydeekewr*
pen	le stylo	*luh steeloa*
pencil	le crayon	*luh krayawn*
penis	le pénis	*luh paynees*
pepper (capsicum)	le poivron	*luh pwahvrawn*
pepper	le poivre	*luh pwahvr*
performance	la représentation de théâtre	*lah ruhprayzohntahsyawn duh tayahtr*

perfume	le parfum	*luh pahrfuhn*
perm (verb)	faire une permanente à	*fehr ewn pehrmahnohnt ah*
perm	la permanente	*lah pehrmahnohnt*
permit	le permis	*luh pehrmee*
person	la personne	*lah pehrson*
personal	personnel	*pehrsonehl*
petrol	l'essence (f.)	*lehssohns*
petrol station	la station-service	*lah stahsyawn sehrvees*
pets	les animaux domestiques	*lay zahneemoa domehsteek*
pharmacy	la pharmacie	*lah fahrmahsee*
phone (by)	par téléphone	*pahr taylayfon*
phone (tele-)	le téléphone	*luh taylayfon*
phone (verb)	téléphoner	*taylayfonay*
phone box	la cabine téléphonique	*lah kahbeen taylayfoneek*
phone directory	l'annuaire	*lahnnewehr*
phone number	le numéro de téléphone	*luh newmayroa duh taylayfon*
photo	la photo	*la foatoa*
photocopier	le photocopieur	*luh foatoakopyuhr*
photocopy (verb)	photocopier	*foatoakopyay*
photocopy	la photocopie	*lah foatoakopee*
pick up	aller chercher	*ahlay shehrshay*
picnic	le pique-nique	*luh peek neek*
pier	la jetée	*lah jhuhtay*
pigeon	le pigeon	*luh peejhyawn*
pill (contraceptive)	la pilule	*lah peelewl*
pillow	le coussin	*luh koossahn*
pillowcase	la taie d'oreiller	*lah tay dorehyay*
pin	l'épingle (f.)	*laypahngl*
pineapple	l'ananas (m.)	*lahnahnahs*
pipe	la pipe	*lah peep*
pipe tobacco	le tabac à pipe	*luh tahbah ah peep*
pity	dommage	*domahjh*
places of entertainment	les possibilités de sortie	*lay poseebeeleetay duh sortee*

places of interest	les curiosités	*lay kewryozeetay*
plan	l'intention (f.)	*lahntohnsyawn*
plant	la plante	*lah plohnt*
plaster	le sparadrap	*luh spahrahdrah*
plastic	plastique	*plahsteek*
plastic bag	le sac en plastique	*luh sahk ohn plahsteek*
plate	l'assiette (f.)	*lahsyeht*
platform	la voie, le quai	*lah vwah, luh kay*
play (theatre)	la pièce de théâtre	*lah pyehs duh tayahtr*
play (verb)	jouer	*jhooay*
play basketball	jouer au basket	*jhooay oa bahskeht*
play billiards	jouer au billiard	*jhooay oa biy-yahr*
play chess	jouer aux échecs	*jhooay oa zayshehk*
play draughts	jouer aux dames	*jhooay oa dahm*
play golf	jouer au golf	*jhooay oa golf*
playing cards	les cartes à jouer	*lay kahrt ah jhooay*
pleasant	agréable	*ahgrayahbl*
please	s'il vous plaît	*seel voo pleh*
pleasure	la satisfaction	*lah sahteesfahksyawn*
plum	la prune	*lah prewn*
pocketknife	le canif	*luh kahneef*
point	indiquer	*ahndeekay*
poison	le poison	*luh pwahzawn*
police	la police	*lah polees*
police station	le poste de police	*luh post duh polees*
policeman	l'agent de police (m.)	*lahjhohn duh polees*
pond	le bassin	*luh bahsahn*
pony	le poney	*luh poaneh*
pop concert	le concert pop	*luh kawnsehr pop*
population	la population	*lah popewlahsyawn*
pork	la viande de porc	*lah vyohnd duh por*
port	le porto	*luh portoa*
porter	le porteur	*luh portuhr*
post code	le code postal	*luh kod postahl*
post office	la poste	*lah post*
postage	le port	*luh por*
postbox	la boîte aux lettres	*lah bwaht oa lehtr*

postcard	la carte postale	*lah kahrt postahl*
postman	le facteur	*luh fahktuhr*
potato	la pomme de terre	*lah pom duh tehr*
poultry	la volaille	*lah vohlahy*
pound	la livre	*lah leevr*
powdered milk	le lait en poudre	*luh leh ohn poodr*
prawns	les crevettes roses	*lay kruhveht roaz*
precious	précieux	*praysyuh*
prefer	préférer	*prayfayray*
preference	la préférence	*lah prayfayrohns*
pregnant	enceinte	*ohnsahnt*
present (adj.)	présent	*prayzohn*
present	le cadeau	*luh kahdoa*
press	appuyer	*ahpweeyay*
pressure	la pression	*lah prehsyawn*
price	le prix	*luh pree*
price list	la liste de prix	*lah leest duh pree*
print (verb)	faire tirer	*fehr teeray*
print	l'épreuve (f.)	*laypruhv*
probably	probablement	*probahbluhmohn*
problem	le problème	*luh problehm*
profession	la profession	*lah profehsyawn*
programme	le programme	*luh prograhm*
pronounce	prononcer	*proanawnsay*
propane gas	le gaz propane	*luh gahz propahn*
pull	arracher	*ahrahshay*
pull a muscle	froisser un muscle	*frwahsay uhn mewskl*
pure	pur	*pewr*
purple	violet	*veeoleh*
purse	le porte-monnaie	*luh port moneh*
push	pousser	*poossay*
pushchair	la poussette	*lah poosseht*
puzzle	le puzzle	*luh puhzl*
pyjamas	le pyjama	*luh peejhahmah*

Q

quarter	le quart	*luh kahr*
quarter of an hour	le quart d'heure	*luh kahr duhr*
queen	la reine	*lah rehn*
question	la question	*lah kehstyawn*
quick	rapide	*rahpeed*
quiet	tranquille	*trohnkeey*

R

radio	la radio	*lah rahdyoa*
railways	les chemins de fer (m.)	*lay shuhmahn duh fehr*
rain (verb)	pleuvoir	*pluhvwahr*
rain	la pluie	*lah plwee*
raincoat	l'imperméable (m.)	*lahnpehrmayahbl*
raisins	les raisins secs	*lay rehzahn sehk*
rape	le viol	*luh vyol*
rapids	le courant rapide	*luh koorohn rahpeed*
raspberries	les framboises	*lay frohnbwahz*
raw	cru	*krew*
raw ham	le jambon cru	*luh jhohnbawn krew*
raw vegetables	les crudités	*lay krewdeetay*
razor blades	les lames de rasoir	*lay lahm duh rahzwahr*
read (verb)	lire	*leer*
ready	prêt	*preh*
really	vraiment	*vrehmohn*
receipt (till)	le ticket de caisse	*luh teekeh duh kehs*
receipt	le reçu, la quittance	*luh ruhsew, lah keetohns*
recipe	la recette	*lah ruhseht*
reclining chair	la chaise longue	*lah shehz lawng*
recommend	recommander	*ruhkomohnday*
recovery service	l'assistance routiere (f.)	*lahseestohns rootyehr*
rectangle	le rectangle	*luh rehktohngl*
red	rouge	*roojh*
red wine	le vin rouge	*luh vahn roojh*
reduction	la réduction	*lah raydewksyawn*

refrigerator	le réfrigérateur	*luh rayfreejhayrahtuhr*
regards	les amitiés	*lay zahmeetyay*
region	la région	*lah rayjhyawn*
registration	la carte grise	*lah kahrt greez*
relatives	la famille	*lah fahmeey*
reliable	sûr	*sewr*
religion	la religion	*lah ruhleejhyawn*
rent out	louer	*looay*
repair (verb)	réparer	*raypahray*
repairs	la réparation	*lah raypahrahsyawn*
repeat	répéter	*raypaytay*
report	le procès-verbal	*luh proseh vehrbahl*
resent	prendre mal	*prohndr mahl*
responsible	responsable	*rehspawnsahbl*
rest	se reposer	*suh ruhpoazay*
restaurant	le restaurant	*luh rehstoarohn*
result	le résultat	*luh rayzewltah*
retired	à la retraite	*ah lah ruhtreht*
retirement	la retraite	*lah ruhtreht*
return (ticket)	l'aller-retour (m.)	*lahlay ruhtoor*
reverse (vehicle)	faire marche arrière	*fehr mahrsh ahryehr*
rheumatism	le rhumatisme	*luh rewmahteesm*
rice	le riz	*luh ree*
ridiculous	ridicule	*reedeekewl*
riding (horseback)	faire du cheval	*fehr dew shuhvahl*
riding school	le manège	*luh mahnehjh*
right	la droite	*lah drwaht*
right of way	la priorité	*lah preeoreetay*
right, on the	à droite	*ah drwaht*
ripe	mûr	*mewr*
risk	le risque	*luh reesk*
river	la rivière	*reevyehr*
road	la route	*lah root*
roasted	rôti	*roatee*
rock	le rocher	*luh roshay*
roll	le petit pain	*luh puhtee pahn*
rolling tobacco	le tabac à rouler	*luh tahbah ah roolay*

roof rack	la galerie	*lah gahlree*
room	la pièce	*lah pyehs*
room number	le numéro de chambre	*luh newmayroa duh shohnbr*
room service	le service de chambre	*luh sehrvees duh shohnbr*
rope	la corde	*lah kord*
rose	la rose	*lah roaz*
rosé	le rosé	*luh roazay*
roundabout	le rond-point	*luh rawn pwahn*
route	l'itinéraire (m.)	*leeteenayrehr*
rowing boat	la barque	*la bahrk*
rubber	le caoutchouc	*luh kah-oochoo*
rubbish	les détritus	*luh daytreetews*
rucksack	le sac à dos	*luh sahk ah doa*
rude	mal élevé	*mahl aylvay*
ruins	les ruines (f.)	*lay rween*
run into	rencontrer	*rohnkawntray*
running shoes	les chaussures de sport	*lay shoasewr duh spor*

S

sad	triste	*treest*
safari	le safari	*luh sahfahree*
safe (adj.)	en sécurité	*ohn saykewreetay*
safe	le coffre-fort	*luh kofr for*
safety pin	l'épingle de nourrice (f.)	*laypahngl duh noorees*
sail	faire de la voile	*fehr duh lah vwahl*
sailing boat	le voilier	*luh vwahlyay*
salad	la salade	*lah sahlahd*
salad oil	l'huile de table (f.)	*lweel duh tahbl*
salami	le salami	*luh sahlahmee*
sale	les soldes	*lay sold*
salt	le sel	*luh sehl*
same	le même	*luh mehm*
sandwich	le sandwich	*luh sohndweech*
sandy beach	la plage de sable	*lah plahhj duh sahbl*
sanitary towel	la serviette hygiénique	*lah sehrvyeht eejhyayneek*

sardines	les sardines	*lay sahrdeen*
satisfied	content (de)	*kawntohn (duh)*
Saturday	samedi	*sahmdee*
sauce	la sauce	*lah soas*
sauna	le sauna	*luh soanah*
sausage	la saucisse	*lah soasees*
savoury	salé	*sahlay*
say	dire	*deer*
scarf	l'écharpe (f.)	*layshahrp*
scenic walk	le circuit pédestre	*luh seerkwee paydehstr*
school	l'école (f.)	*laykol*
scissors	les ciseaux	*lay seezoa*
scooter	le scooter	*luh skootehr*
scorpion	le scorpion	*luh skorpyawn*
Scotland	l'Ecosse (f.)	*laykos*
Scottish	écossais	*aykosseh*
scrambled eggs	l'oeuf brouillé (m.)	*lef brooy-yay*
screw	la vis	*lah vees*
screwdriver	le tournevis	*luh toornuhvees*
sculpture	la sculpture	*lah skewltewr*
sea	la mer	*lah mehr*
seasick (to be)	avoir le mal de mer	*ahvwahr luh mahl duh mehr*
seat	la place	*lah plahs*
second-hand	d'occasion	*dokahzyawn*
second (adj.)	deuxième	*duhzyehm*
second	la seconde	*lah suhgawnd*
sedative	le tranquillisant	*luh trohnkeeleezohn*
self-timer	le déclencheur	*luh dayklohnshuhr*
	automatique	*oatoamahteek*
semi-skimmed	demi-écrémé	*duhmee aykraymay*
send	expédier	*ehxpaydyay*
sentence	la phrase	*lah frahz*
separated	séparé	*saypahray*
September	septembre	*sehptohnbr*
serious	sérieux	*sayryuh*
service	le service	*luh sehrvees*
serviette	la serviette	*lah sehrvyeht*

set (hair)	faire une mise en plis	*fehr ewn meez ohn plee*
sewing thread	le fil à coudre	*luh feel ah koodr*
shade	l'ombre (f.)	*lawnbr*
shallow	peu profond	*puh profawn*
shampoo	le shampooing	*luh shohnpwahn*
shark	le requin	*luh ruhkahn*
shave (verb)	se raser	*suh rahzay*
shaver	le rasoir électrique	*luh rahzwahr aylehktreek*
shaving brush	le blaireau	*luh blayroa*
shaving cream	la crème à raser	*lah krehm ah rahzay*
shaving soap	le savon à raser	*luh sahvawn ah rahzay*
sheet	le drap	*luh drah*
sherry	le xérès	*luh ksayrehz*
shirt	la chemise	*lah shuhmeez*
shoe	la chaussure	*lah shoasewr*
shoe polish	le cirage	*luh seerajh*
shoe shop	le magasin de chaussures	*luh mahgahzahn duh shoasewr*
shoelace	le lacet	*luh lahseh*
shoemaker	le cordonnier	*luh kordonyay*
shop (verb)	faire les courses	*fehr lay koors*
shop	le magasin	*luh mahgahzahn*
shop assistant	la vendeuse	*lah vohnduhz*
shop window	la vitrine	*lah veetreen*
shopping bag	le cabas	*luh kahbah*
shopping centre	le centre commercial	*luh sohntr komehrsyahl*
short	court	*koor*
short circuit	le court-circuit	*luh koor seerkwee*
shorts	le bermuda	*luh behrmewdah*
shoulder	l'épaule (f.)	*laypoal*
show	le spectacle	*luh spehktahkl*
shower	la douche	*lah doosh*
shutter	l'obturateur (m.)	*lobtewrahtuhr*
sieve	la passoire	*lah pahswahr*
sign (verb)	signer	*seenyay*
sign	le panneau	*luh pahnoa*
signature	la signature	*lah seenyahtewr*

silence	le silence	*luh seelohns*
silver	l'argent (m.)	*lahrjhohn*
silver-plated	argenté	*ahrjhohntay*
simple	simple	*sahnpl*
single (ticket)	l'aller simple (m.)	*lahlay sahnpl*
single (unmarried)	célibataire	*sayleebahtehr*
single	le célibataire	*luh sayleebahtehr*
sir	monsieur	*muhsyuh*
sister	la soeur	*lah suhr*
sit (verb)	s'asseoir	*sahswahr*
size	la pointure, la taille	*lah pwahntewr, lah tahy*
ski (verb)	skier, faire du ski	*skeeay, fehr dew skee*
ski boots	les chaussures de ski	*lay shoasewr duh skee*
ski goggles	les lunettes de ski	*lay lewneht duh skee*
ski instructor	le moniteur de ski	*luh moneetuhr duh skee*
ski lessons/class	le cours de ski,	*luh koor duh skee,*
	la classe de ski	*lah klahs duh skee*
ski lift	le remonte-pente	*luh ruhmawnt pohnt*
ski pants	le pantalon de ski	*luh pohntahlawn duh skee*
ski pass	le forfait de ski	*luh forfeh duh skee*
ski slope	la piste de ski	*lah peest duh skee*
ski stick	le bâton de ski	*luh bahtawn duh skee*
ski suit	la combinaison	*lah kawnbeeneh-*
	de ski	*zawn duh skee*
ski wax	le fart à ski	*luh fahr ah skee*
skimmed	écrémé	*aykraymay*
skin	la peau	*lah poa*
skirt	la jupe	*lah jhewp*
skis	les skis	*lay skee*
sledge	la luge	*lah lewjh*
sleep (verb)	dormir	*dormeer*
sleep well	dormez-bien	*dormay byahn*
sleeping car	le wagon-lit	*luh vahgawn lee*
sleeping pills	les somnifères	*lay somneefehr*
slide	la diapositive	*lah deeahpozeeteev*
slim	mince	*mahns*
slip	la combinaison	*lah kawnbeenehzawn*

slip road	la bretelle d'accès	*lah bruhtehl dahkseh*
slow	lentement	*lohntuhmohn*
small	petit	*puhtee*
small change	la monnaie	*lah moneh*
smell (verb)	puer	*peway*
smoke	la fumée	*lah fewmay*
smoke (verb)	fumer	*fewmay*
smoked	fumé	*fewmay*
smoking compartment	le compartiment fumeurs	*luh kawnpahrteemohn fewmuhr*
snake	le serpent	*luh sehrpohn*
snorkel	le tuba	*luh tewbah*
snow (verb)	neiger	*nchjhay*
snow	la neige	*lah nehjh*
snow chains	les chaînes	*lay shehn*
soap	le savon	*luh sahvawn*
soap box	la boîte à savon	*lah bwaht ah sahvawn*
soccer (play)	jouer au football, le football	*jhooay oa footbol, luh footbol*
soccer match	le match de football	*luh mahch duh footbol*
socket	la prise	*lah preez*
socks	les chaussettes	*lay shoasseht*
soft drink	la boisson fraîche	*lah bwahssawn frehsh*
sole (fish)	la sole	*lah sol*
sole (shoe)	la semelle	*lah suhmehl*
solicitor	l'avocat	*lahvoakah*
someone	quelqu'un	*kehlkuhn*
something	quelque chose	*kehlkuhshoaz*
sometimes	parfois	*pahrfwah*
somewhere	quelque part	*kehlkuhpahr*
son	le fils	*luh fees*
soon	bientôt	*byahntoa*
sorbet	le sorbet	*luh sorbeh*
sore (be)	faire mal	*fehr mal*
sore throat	le mal de gorge	*luh mahl duh gorjh*
sorry	pardon	*pahrdawn*
sort	la sorte	*lah sort*

soup	la soupe	*lah soop*
sour	acide	*ahseed*
sour cream	la crème fraîche	*lah krehm frehsh*
source	la source	*lah soors*
south	le sud	*luh sewd*
souvenir	le souvenir	*luh soovneer*
spaghetti	les spaghetti	*lay spahgehtee*
spanner (open-ended)	las clé plate	*lay klay plaht*
spanner	la clef à molette	*lah klay ah moleht*
spare parts	les pièces détachées	*lay pyehs daytashay*
spare tyre	le pneu de rechange	*luh pnuh duh ruhshohnjh*
spare wheel	la roue de secours	*lah roo duh suhkoor*
speak (verb)	parler	*pahrlay*
special	spécial	*spaysyahl*
specialist	le spécialiste	*luh spaysyahleest*
specialty	la spécialité	*lah spaysyahleetay*
speed limit	la vitesse maximum	*lah veetehs mahxeemuhm*
spell (verb)	épeler	*aypuhlay*
spices	les épices	*lay zaypees*
spicy	épicé	*aypeesay*
splinter	l'écharde (f.)	*layshahrd*
spoon	la cuillère	*lah kweeyehr*
spoonful	la cuillerée	*lah kweeyuhray*
sport	le sport	*luh spor*
sports centre	la salle de sport	*lah sahl duh spohr*
spot	l'endroit (m.)	*lohndrwah*
sprain	fouler	*foolay*
spring	le printemps	*luh prahntohn*
square	le carré	*luh kahray*
square (town)	la place	*lah plahs*
square metre	le mètre carré	*luh mehtr kahray*
squash	le squash	*luh skwahsh*
stadium	le stade	*luh stahd*
stain	la tache	*lah tahsh*
stain remover	le détachant	*luh daytahshohn*
stairs	l'escalier (m.)	*lehskahlyay*

stalls	la salle	*lah sahl*
stamp	le timbre	*luh tahnbr*
start (verb)	démarrer	*daymahray*
station	la gare	*lah gahr*
statue	la statue	*lah stahtew*
stay (lodge)	loger	*lohjhay*
stay (remain)	rester	*rehstay*
stay	le séjour	*luh sayjhoor*
steal	voler	*volay*
steel	acier	*ahsyay*
stench	la mauvaise odeur	*lah moavehz oduhr*
sting	piquer	*peekay*
stitch (med.)	la suture	*lah sewtewr*
stitch (verb)	suturer	*sewtewray*
stock	le consommé	*luh kawnsomay*
stockings	les bas	*lay bah*
stomach	l'estomac (m.)	*lehstomah*
stomach	le ventre	*luh vohntr*
stomach ache	mal au ventre	*mahl oa vohntr*
stomach ache	le mal d'estomac	*luh mahl dehstomah*
stomach cramps	les spasmes abdominaux	*lay spahzm zahbdomeenoa*
stools	les selles	*lay sehl*
stop	arrêter	*ahrehtay*
stop	l'arrêt (m.)	*lahreh*
stopover	l'escale (f.)	*lehskahl*
storm	la tempête	*lah tohnpeht*
straight	raide	*rehd*
straight ahead	tout droit	*too drwah*
straw	la paille	*lah pahy*
street	la rue	*lah rew*
street (side)	côté rue	*koatay rew*
strike	la grève	*lah grehv*
study	faire des études	*fehr day zaytewd*
subscriber's number	le numéro d'abonné	*luh newmayroa dahbonay*
subtitled	sous-titré	*soo teetray*

succeed	réussir	*rayewsseer*
sugar	le sucre	*luh sewkr*
sugar lumps	les morceaux de sucre	*lay morsoa duh sewkr*
suit	le costume	*luh kostewm*
suitcase	la valise	*lah vahleez*
summer	l'été (m.)	*laytay*
summertime	l'heure d'été (f.)	*luhr daytay*
sun	le soleil	*luh solehy*
sun hat	le chapeau de soleil	*luh shahpoa duh solehy*
sun hat	le bonnet	*luh boneh*
sunbathe	prendre un bain de soleil	*prohndr uhn bahn duh solehy*
sunburn	le coup de soleil	*luh koo duh solehy*
Sunday	dimanche	*deemohnsh*
sunglasses	les lunettes de soleil	*lay lewneht duh solehy*
sunrise	le lever du soleil	*luh luhvay duh solehy*
sunset	le coucher du soleil	*luh kooshay duh solehy*
suntan lotion	la crème solaire	*lah krehm solehr*
suntan oil	l'huile solaire (f.)	*lweel sohlehr*
supermarket	le supermarché	*luh sewpehrmahrshay*
surcharge	le supplément	*luh sewplaymohn*
surf board	la planche à voile	*lah plohnsh ah vwahl*
surgery	la consultation	*lah kawnsewltahsyawn*
surname	le nom	*luh nawn*
surprise	la surprise	*lah sewrpreez*
swallow	avaler	*ahvahlay*
swamp	le marais	*luh mahreh*
sweat	la transpiration	*lah trohnspeerahsyawn*
sweet	le bonbon	*luh bawnbawn*
sweet (kind)	gentil	*jhohntee*
sweet (adj.)	sucré	*sewkray*
sweetcorn	le maïs	*luh mahees*
sweets	les friandises	*lay freeohndeez*
swim	nager	*nahjhay*
swimming pool	la piscine	*lah peeseen*
swimming trunks	le maillot de bain	*luh mahyoa duh bahn*
swindle	l'escroquerie (f.)	*lehskrokree*

| switch | l'interrupteur (m.) | *lahntayrewptuhr* |
| synagogue | la synagogue | *lah seenahgog* |

T

table	la table	*lah tahbl*
table tennis	jouer au ping-pong	*jhooay oa peeng pawng*
tablet	le comprimé	*luh kawnpreemay*
take (use)	utiliser	*ewteeleezay*
take	prendre	*prohndr*
take (time)	durer	*dewray*
take pictures	photographier	*foatoagrahfyay*
taken	occupé	*okewpay*
talcum powder	le talc	*luh tahlk*
talk	parler	*pahrlay*
tall	grand	*grohn*
tampons	les tampons	*lay tohnpawn*
tanned	brun	*bruhn*
tap	le robinet	*luh robeeneh*
tap water	l'eau du robinet (f.)	*loa dew robeeneh*
tartlet	la tartelette	*lah tahrtuhleht*
taste	goûter	*gootay*
tax free shop	le magasin hors-taxes	*luh mahgahzahn or tahx*
taxi	le taxi	*luh tahxee*
taxi stand	la station de taxis	*lah stahsyawn duh tahxee*
tea	le thé	*luh tay*
teapot	la théière	*lah tay-yehr*
teaspoon	la petite cuillère	*lah puhteet kweeyehr*
telegram	le télégramme	*luh taylaygrahm*
telephoto lens	le téléobjectif	*luh taylayobjhehkteef*
television	la télévision	*lah taylayveezyawn*
telex	le télex	*luh taylehx*
temperature	la température	*lah tohnpayrahtewr*
temporary filling	le plombage provisoire	*luh plawnbahjh proveezwahr*
tender	tendre	*tohndr*
tennis (play)	jouer au tennis	*jhooay oa taynees*
tennis ball	la balle de tennis	*lah bahl duh taynees*

tennis court	le court de tennis	*luh koor duh taynees*
tennis racket	la raquette de tennis	*lah rahkeht duh taynees*
tent	la tente	*lah tohnt*
tent peg	le piquet	*luh peekay*
terrace	la terrasse	*lah tehrahs*
terrible	épouvantable	*aypoovohntahbl*
thank	remercier	*ruhmehrsyay*
thank you	merci bien	*mehrsee byahn*
thanks	merci	*mehrsee*
thaw	dégeler	*dayjhuhlay*
theatre	le théâtre	*luh tayahtr*
theft	le vol	*luh vol*
there	là	*lah*
thermal bath	le bain thermal	*luh bahn tehrmahl*
thermometer	le thermomètre	*luh tehrmomehtr*
thick	gros	*groa*
thief	le voleur	*luh voluhr*
thigh	la cuisse	*lah kwees*
thin	maigre	*mehgr*
think	penser	*pohnsay*
third	le tiers	*luh tyehr*
thirsty, to be	la soif	*lah swahf*
this afternoon	cet après-midi	*seht ahpreh meedee*
this evening	ce soir	*suh swahr*
this morning	ce matin	*suh mahtahn*
thread	le fil	*luh feel*
throat	la gorge	*lah gorjh*
throat lozenges	les pastilles	*lay pahsteey*
	pour la gorge	*poor lah gorjh*
throw up	vomir	*vomeer*
thunderstorm	l'orage (m.)	*lorajh*
Thursday	jeudi	*jhuhdee*
ticket (admission)	le billet	*luh beeyeh*
ticket (travel)	le ticket	*luh teekeh*
tickets	les billets	*lay beeyeh*
tidy	ranger	*rohnjhay*
tie	la cravate	*lah krahvaht*

tights	le collant	*luh kolohn*
time (clock)	l'heure (f.)	*luhr*
time (occasion)	la fois	*lah fwah*
timetable	l'horaire des arrivées	*lorehr day zahreevay*
	et des départs	*ay day daypahr*
tin	la boîte de conserve	*lah bwaht duh kawnsehrv*
tip	le pourboire	*luh poorbwahr*
tissues	les mouchoirs en papier	*lay mooshwahr ohn*
		pahpyay
toast	le toast	*luh toast*
tobacco	le tabac	*luh tahbah*
toboggan	la luge	*lah lewjh*
today	aujourd'hui	*oajhoordwee*
toe	l'orteil (m.)	*lortehy*
together	ensemble	*ohnsohnbl*
toilet	les toilettes	*lay twahleht*
toilet paper	le papier hygiénique	*luh pahpyay eejhyayneek*
toiletries	les articles de toilette	*lay zahrteekl duh twahleht*
tomato	la tomate	*lah tomaht*
tomato purée	le concentré	*luh kawnsohntray*
	de tomates	*duh tomaht*
tomato sauce	le ketchup	*luh kehtchuhp*
tomorrow	demain	*duhmahn*
tongue	la langue	*lah lohng*
tonic water	le tonic	*luh toneek*
tonight	ce soir	*suh swahr*
tonight	cette nuit	*seht nwee*
too much	trop	*troa*
tools	les outils	*lay zootee*
tooth	la dent	*lah dohn*
toothache	le mal de dents	*luh mahl duh dohn*
toothbrush	la brosse à dents	*lah bros ah dohn*
toothpaste	le dentifrice	*luh dohnteefrees*
toothpick	le cure-dent	*luh kewrdohn*
top up	remplir	*rohnpleer*
total	le total	*luh totahl*
tough	dur	*dewr*

tour	le tour	*luh toor*
tour guide	le guide	*luh geed*
tourist card	la carte touristique	*lah kahrt tooreesteek*
tourist class	la classe touriste	*lah klahs tooreest*
Tourist Information office	l'office de tourisme	*lofees duh tooreesm*
tow	remorquer	*ruhmorkay*
tow cable	le câble	*luh kahbl*
towel	la serviette de toilette	*lah sehrvyeht duh twahleht*
tower	la tour	*lah toor*
town	la ville	*lah veel*
town hall	la mairie	*lah mayree*
toy	le jouet	*luh jhooeh*
traffic	la circulation	*lah seerkewlahsyawn*
traffic light	le feu de signalisation	*luh fuh duh seenyahleezahsyawn*
train	le train	*luh trahn*
train ticket	le billet de train	*luh beeyeh duh trahn*
train timetable	l'indicateur des chemins de fer	*lahndeekahtuhr day shuhmahn duh fehr*
translate	traduire	*trahdweer*
travel	voyager	*vwahyahjhay*
travel agent	l'agence de voyages (f.)	*lahjhohns duh vwahyahjh*
travel guide	le guide touristique	*luh geed tooreesteek*
traveller	le voyageur	*luh vwahyahjhuhr*
traveller's cheque	le chèque de voyage	*luh shehk duh vwahyahjh*
treacle	la mélasse	*lah maylahs*
treatment	le traitement	*luh trehtmohn*
triangle	le triangle	*luh treeohngl*
trim	tailler	*tahy-yay*
trip	l'excursion (f.)	*lehxkewrsyawn*
trip	le voyage	*luh vwahyahjh*
trout	la truite	*lah trweet*
trunk call	interurbain	*ahntehrewrbahn*

trunk code	l'indicatif (m.)	*lahndeekahteef*
trustworthy	de confiance	*duh kawnfyohns*
try on	essayer	*ehsay-yay*
tube	le tube	*luh tewb*
Tuesday	mardi	*mahrdee*
tumble drier	le sèche-linge	*luh sahsh lahnjh*
tuna	le thon	*luh tawn*
tunnel	le tunnel	*luh tewnehl*
TV	la télé	*lah taylay*
tweezers	la pince	*lah pahns*
tyre	le pneu	*luh pnuh*
tyre lever	le démonte-pneu	*luh daymawnt pnuh*
tyre pressure	la pression des pneus	*lah prehsyawn day pnuh*

U

ugly	laid	*leh*
umbrella	le parapluie	*luh pahrahplwee*
under	sous	*soo*
underground	le métro	*luh maytroa*
underground railway system	le réseau métropolitain	*luh rayzoa maytroapoleetahn*
underground station	la station de métro	*lah stahsyawn duh maytroa*
underpants	le slip	*luh sleep*
understand	comprendre	*kawnprohndr*
underwear	les sous-vêtements	*lay soovehtmohn*
undress	(se) déshabiller	*suh dayzahbeeyay*
unemployed	au chômage	*oa shoamahjh*
uneven	irrégulier	*eeraygewlyay*
university	l'université (f.)	*lewneevehrseetay*
unleaded	sans plomb	*sohn plawn*
up	en haut	*ohn oa*
urgent	urgent	*ewrjhohn*
urine	l'urine (f.)	*lewreen*
usually	généralement	*jhaynayrahlmohn*

vacate	évacuer	*ayvahkeway*
vaccinate	vacciner	*vahkseenay*
vagina	le vagin	*luh vahjhahn*
vaginal infection	l'infection vaginale	*lahnfehksyawn vahjheenahl*
valid	valable	*vahlahbl*
valley	la vallée	*lah vahlay*
van	la camionnette	*lah kahmyoneht*
vanilla	la vanille	*lah vahneey*
vase	le vase	*luh vahz*
vaseline	la vaseline	*lah vahzleen*
veal	la viande de veau	*lah vyohnd duh voa*
vegetable soup	la soupe de légumes	*lah soop duh laygewm*
vegetables	le légume	*luh laygewm*
vegetarian	le végétarien	*luh vayjhaytahryahn*
vein	la veine	*lah vehn*
vending machine	le distributeur	*luh deestreebewtuhr*
venereal disease	la maladie vénérienne	*lah mahlahdee vaynayryehn*
via	par	*pahr*
video recorder	le magnétoscope	*luh manyehtoskop*
video tape	la bande vidéo	*lah bohnd veedayoa*
view	la vue	*lah vew*
village	le village	*luh veelahjh*
visa	le visa	*luh veezah*
visit (verb)	rendre visite à	*rohndr veezeet ah*
visit	la visite	*lah veezeet*
vitamin tablet	le comprimé de vitamines	*luh kawnpreemay duh veetahmeen*
vitamin	la vitamine	*lah veetahmeen*
volcano	le volcan	*luh volkohn*
volleyball	jouer au volley	*jhooay oa volay*
vomit	vomir	*vomeer*

wait	attendre	*ahtohndr*
waiter	le serveur	*luh sehrvuhr*
waiting room	la salle d'attente	*lah sahl dahtohnt*
waitress	la serveuse	*lah sehrvuhz*
wake up	réveiller	*rayvay-yay*
walk	la promenade	*lah promnahd*
walk (verb)	se promener marcher	*suh promnay mahrshay*
wallet	le portefeuille	*luh portuhfuhy*
wardrobe	la garde-robe	*lah gahrd rob*
warm	chaud	*shoa*
warn	prévenir	*prayvuhneer*
warning	l'avertissement (m.)	*lahvehrteesmohn*
wash	laver	*lahvay*
washing-powder	le détergent	*luh daytehrjhohn*
washing	le linge	*luh lahnjh*
washing line	la corde à linge	*lah kord ah lahnjh*
washing machine	la machine à laver	*lah mahsheen ah lahvay*
wasp	la guêpe	*lah gehp*
water	l'eau (f.)	*loa*
water ski	faire du ski nautique	*fehr dew skee noateek*
waterproof	imperméable	*ahnpehrmayahbl*
wave-pool	la piscine à vagues artificielles	*lah peeseen ah vahg zahrteefeesyehl*
way	le moyen	*luh mwahyahn*
way	la direction	*lah deerehksyawn*
we	nous	*noo*
weak	faible	*fehbl*
weather	le temps	*luh tohn*
weather forecast	le bulletin météorologique	*luh bewltahn maytayoarolojheek*
wedding	les noces	*lay nos*
wedding	le mariage	*luh mahryajh*
Wednesday	mercredi	*mehrkruhdee*
week	la semaine	*lah suhmehn*
weekend	le week-end	*luh week-ehnd*

English	French	Pronunciation
weekend duty	le service de garde	*luh sehrvees duh gahrd*
weekly ticket	l'abonnement hebdomadaire (m.)	*lahbonmohn ehbdomahdehr*
welcome	bienvenu	*byahnvuhnew*
well	bien	*byahn*
west	l'ouest (m.)	*lwehst*
wet	humide	*ewmeed*
wetsuit	la combinaison de planche à voile	*lah kawnbeenehzawn duh plohnsh ah vwahl*
what?	quoi?	*kwah?*
wheel	la roue	*lah roo*
wheelchair	la chaise roulante	*lah shehz roolohnt*
when?	quand?	*kohn?*
where?	où?	*oo?*
which?	quel?	*kehl?*
whipped cream	la crème Chantilly	*lah krehm shohnteeyee*
white	blanc	*blohn*
who?	qui?	*kee?*
wholemeal bread	le pain complet	*luh pahn kawnpleh*
why?	pourquoi?	*poorkwah?*
wide-angle lens	le grand-angle	*luh grohn tohngl*
widow	la veuve	*lah vuhv*
widower	le veuf	*luh vuhf*
wife	l'épouse (f.)	*laypooz*
wind	le vent	*luh vohn*
windbreak	le pare-vent	*luh pahrvohn*
windmill	le moulin	*luh moolahn*
window (desk)	le guichet	*luh gueesheh*
window	la fenêtre	*lah fuhnehtr*
windscreen wiper	l'essuie-glace (m.)	*lehswee glahs*
windsurf	faire de la planche à voile	*fehr duh lah plohnsh ah vwahl*
wine	le vin	*luh vahn*
wine list	la carte des vins	*lah kahrt day vahn*
winter	l'hiver (m.)	*leevehr*
witness	le témoin	*luh taymwahn*
woman	la femme	*lah fahm*

wood	le bois	*luh bwah*
wool	la laine	*lah lehn*
word	le mot	*luh moa*
work	le travail	*luh trahvahy*
working day	le jour ouvrable	*jhoor oovrahbl*
worn	usé	*ewzay*
worried	inquiet	*ahnkyeh*
wound	la blessure	*lah blehsewr*
wrap	emballer	*ohnbahlay*
wrist	le poignet	*luh pwahnnyeh*
write	écrire	*aykreer*
write down	noter	*notay*
writing pad	le bloc-notes	*luh blok not*
writing paper	le papier à lettres	*luh pahpyay ah lehtr*
written	écrit	*aykree*
wrong	mauvais	*moaveh*

Y

yacht	le yacht	*luh yot*
year	l'année (f.)	*lahnay*
yellow	jaune	*jhoan*
yes	oui	*wee*
yes, please	volontiers	*volawntyay*
yesterday	hier	*yehr*
yoghurt	le yaourt	*luh yahoort*
you	vous	*voo*
you too	de même	*duh mehm*
youth hostel	l'auberge de jeunesse (f.)	*loabehrjh duh jhuhnehs*

Z

| zip | la fermeture éclair | *lah fehrmuhtewr ayklehr* |
| zoo | le parc zoologique | *luh pahrk zoaolojheek* |

1 The article

French nouns are divided into 2 categories: masculine and feminine. The definite article (the) is **le, la** or **l'**:

le is used before masculine words starting with a consonant, **le magasin** (the shop)

la is used with feminine words starting with a consonant, **la plage** (the beach)

l' is used before masculine and feminine words starting with a vowel, **l'argent** (the money), **l'assiette** (the plate).

Other examples are:

le toit	the roof
la maison	the house
l'hôtel (m.)	the hotel
l'entrée (f.)	the entrance

in the case of the indefinite article (**a, an**):

un is used before masculine words, **un livre** (a book)

une is used before feminine words, **une pomme** (an apple)

des is used before plural words, both masculine and feminine, **des camions** (lorries), **des voitures** (cars).

Other examples are:

un père	a father	**une mère**	a mother
un homme	a man	**une femme**	a woman
des hommes	men	**des femmes**	women

2 The plural

The plural of **le**, **la** and **l'** is **les**.
The plural of most French nouns ends in **s**, but this **s** is not pronounced. However when the noun begins with a vowel or a silent **h**, then the **s** of **les** or **des** is pronounced **z, les affaires** (*layzahfehr*), **des enfants** (*dayzohngfohn*).

Other examples are:

le lit	*luh lee*	**les lits**	*lay lee*
la table	*lah tahbl*	**les tables**	*lay tahbl*
l'avion (m.)	*lahveeawn*	**les avions**	*layzahvyeeawn*
l'heure (f.)	*luhr*	**les heures**	*layzuhr*

Certain plurals end in **aux** (mainly words ending in '**al**')
le cheval   **les chevaux**
le canal   **les canaux**

3 Personal pronouns

I	**je**
You	**tu**
He/she/it	**il/elle**
We	**nous**
You	**vous**
They	**ils/elles**

In general '**tu**' is used to translate 'you' when speaking to close friends, relatives and children. **Vous** is used in all other cases. 'It' becomes **il** or **elle** according to whether the noun referred to is masculine or feminine.

4 Possessive pronouns

	masculine	feminine	plural
my	**mon**	**ma**	**mes**
your	**ton**	**ta**	**tes**
his/her/its	**son**	**sa**	**ses**
our	**notre**	**notre**	**nos**
your	**votre**	**votre**	**vos**
their	**leur**	**leur**	**leurs**

They agree with the object they refer to, e.g. her hat = **son chapeau**.

5 Verbs

parler		to speak
je parle	root + -e	I speak
tu parles	root + -es	you speak
il/elle parle	root + -e	he/she/it speaks
nous parlons	root + -ons	we speak
vous parlez	root + -ez	you speak
ils/elles parlent	root + -ent	they speak
parlé (past participle)		spoken

Here are some useful verbs.

être	to be
je suis	I am
tu es	you are
il/elle est	he/she/it is
nous sommes	we are
vous êtes	you are
ils/elles sont	they are
été (past participle)	been

avoir	to have
j'ai	I have
tu as	you have
il/elle a	he/she/it has
nous avons	we have
vous avez	you have
ils/elles ont	they have
eu (past participle)	had

faire	to do/make
je fais	I do
tu fais	you do
il/elle fait	he/she does
nous faisons	we do
vous faites	you do
ils/elles font	they do
fait (past participle)	done/made

6 Countries and prepositions

Names of countries take the article:

L'Angleterre	England
Le Canada	Canada
La France	France

in Paris	**à Paris**
in France	**en France**
in Canada	**au Canada**

7 Negatives

Negatives are formed by using:

ne (verb) **pas**	not
ne (verb) **jamais**	never

Je ne parle pas français.	I don't speak French.
Je ne fume jamais.	I never smoke.